Testimony and Trauma

Testimony and Trauma

Making Space for Healing

Amanda Hontz Drury

LEXINGTON BOOKS/FORTRESS ACADEMIC
Lanham • Boulder • New York • London

Published by Lexington Books/Fortress Academic
Lexington Books is an imprint of The Rowman & Littlefield Publishing Group, Inc.
4501 Forbes Boulevard, Suite 200, Lanham, Maryland 20706
www.rowman.com

86-90 Paul Street, London EC2A 4NE, United Kingdom

Copyright © 2021 The Rowman & Littlefield Publishing Group, Inc.

All rights reserved. No part of this book may be reproduced in any form or by any electronic or mechanical means, including information storage and retrieval systems, without written permission from the publisher, except by a reviewer who may quote passages in a review.

British Library Cataloguing in Publication Information Available

Library of Congress Cataloging-in-Publication Data

Names: Hontz Drury, Amanda, 1981- author.
Title: Testimony and trauma : making space for healing / Amanda Hontz Drury.
Description: Lanham, Maryland : Lexington Books/Fortress Academic, [2021] | Includes bibliographical references and index. | Summary: "Testimony and Trauma explores the Christian practice of testimony through the lens of articulation theory in order to facilitate healing"—Provided by publisher.
Identifiers: LCCN 2021032998 (print) | LCCN 2021032999 (ebook) | ISBN 9781978707719 (cloth) | ISBN 9781978707726 (epub)
Subjects: LCSH: Abused women—Religious life. | Sexual abuse victims—Religious life. | Witness bearing (Christianity) | Psychic trauma—Religious aspects—Christianity. | Spiritual healing.
Classification: LCC BV4596.A2 H66 2021 (print) | LCC BV4596.A2 (ebook) | DDC 261.8/3272—dc23
LC record available at https://lccn.loc.gov/2021032998
LC ebook record available at https://lccn.loc.gov/2021032999

In Gratitude. . .
To the women who graciously shared their stories with me. Thank you for your grace and your courage.
Peace.

Contents

Acknowledgments	ix
1 Testimony and Trauma	1
Theological Interlude 1: Christ has died. Christ has risen. Trauma will come again.	19
2 The Ten Women	27
Theological Interlude 2: Feeding the Enemy	47
3 Event: Jacob's Story	49
Theological Interlude 3: Jesus Weeps	61
4 Articulation: Karen's Story	63
Theological Interlude 4: Clinging to the Dead	79
5 Recognition: Rachel's Story	81
Theological Interlude 5: Running	97
Conclusion	99
Bibliography	101
Index	105
About the Author	107

Acknowledgments

I'm grateful for the three women and their families who so graciously shared with me some of their most raw and painful stories. In addition to your trust, you gave me hours and hours of your time. Your names may not appear in this manuscript, but your stories of trauma intermingled with hope are a blessing.

I'm grateful for colleagues and friends at Indiana Wesleyan University who helped me protect writing time and encouraged me along the way. And thanks to Elaine, who was my motivational coach every time I was anxious about pressing "send" on a draft.

While I am no longer in Stuart Hall taking classes at Princeton Theological Seminary, I continue to learn and grow from a stellar faculty. Thanks to Rick Osmer—I did not anticipate how our conversations on articulation theory would shape so much of my subsequent scholarship. And thanks to Gordon Mikoski—every time I read through this manuscript, I see just how influential you have been in directing my learning and sparking ideas. And thank you in particular for the conversation in 90-degree weather on the Princeton University campus—I doubt you know just how important that conversation was for me. Thank you, Deborah van Deusen Hunsinger, for sharing your syllabi and allowing me to "read along from home" (any mistakes are my own). Thank you for allowing your life to deeply shape the way you teach. I'm having a difficult time articulating just how blessed I have been both by your friendship and by your teaching. I'm still a bit in awe that you would spend hours on the phone with me talking through these ideas. Your presence and your expertise have been a pure gift in my life, and I will always delight in being your student.

Thank you to Kenda for your timely questions and thoughtful words of encouragement—you are mentor and friend all wrapped into one. Thanks,

Felicia, for your counsel and words of healing—I didn't know that was possible. Wendy—thanks for the unexpected beauty you infused into my life. I'm so glad we survived the taxi ride to Eindhoven. And thank you, Kristine, for your presence. I am blessed to have a friend who is also so skilled in pastoral care.

My deepest gratitude to the woman who helped me choose life and who bolstered my faith—Judy, thank you for the times you "dropped everything" to minister to me. You embodied the church for me during a painful period of my life. Thank you for being my confidant, director, and friend. I think you've been at every fork in the road within my adult life—listening, encouraging, and praying. You have blessed me immensely.

Thank you to my extended family whose fingerprints can be seen all throughout this book. The prayers you said, the permission you gave, and the encouragement you offered are gifts beyond measure. In particular, I'd like to thank my parents, Marilyn and Paul Hontz. You have prayed for me, encouraged me, and shared your own learning as I've delved into this book. You have given so freely of your own life experience, and I am so grateful to be your daughter. And thank you, Andra, for all you did to keep us all up and running. As Clara says, "She's just like one of the family."

Thanks to my children: Samuel, Clara, and Paul. Thanks for your understanding and encouragement as I've been writing. Paul, you were not born when this project began, and your debut near the start added so much joy and life to our family.

Finally, thank you to John. I'm grateful for the generative conversations on Hegel and Judith Butler (any mistakes in this book are entirely my own and would be in spite of his theological musings). Thank you for those many times when out of the blue you said things like, "Why don't you take 24 hours away to write" and "Why don't you take 24-hours away and *not* write." While my words of appreciation could continue on from here, I will conclude by thanking you for that period of time when you carried alongside me that which I found so unbearable. This was the kind of love that lays down its life for its friend.

Chapter 1

Testimony and Trauma

This story begins with a piece of hate mail. My husband used to tease me about my eagerness to check the mailbox. While I knew bills were likely, I always held out hope for an unexpected invitation or a forgotten package ordered online—I loved the mail.

The surprise in the mail on this particular day, however, was certainly not a pleasant one. It was anonymous (as much hate mail seems to be), and it was vicious. I only read the letter once, but there are still snippets engraved in my brain. "Your ugly sin," was one line. Another instructed me to "Repent!!!" with multiple exclamation points.

Earlier that summer my extended family suffered a blow. It was one of those stories involving ministry and scandal, and it played itself out in the public eye.[1] I was unaware of the role I played in the saga until much later in the game, but I emerged feeling powerless, used, and very foolish. Though I was on the periphery of this ordeal, I was nevertheless included in the shame that ensued. Friendships were lost and speaking engagements were canceled, but it was this single letter that seemed to get to me the most. While it is still unclear to me just what my "ugly sin" was in this event, the remark prompted me to shrink under the shame.

"You have to just throw stuff like that away," came the response of a well-meaning friend when I shared with her the contents of the letter. But it wasn't that simple. I could dismiss the hateful words, but what really got to me were all of the other people who must be thinking the *exact same things* as the letter writer but were just too polite to say so. Even worse, during my particularly low moments, the voices in my head agreed with the painful missive.

That letter ended my playful relationship with the postal service. Instead of excitement, the postal service now evoked feelings of dread. I would hear the mail truck, and my breathing would become ragged. I went days without opening my mailbox. On top of it all, I was deeply embarrassed. I was ashamed that I could be so thrown off by a single letter. I was ashamed by how much power seemed to reside within that small white truck. My seemingly out-of-proportion response to the postal service indicated to me a weakness of character and a penchant for the dramatic. It was a *letter*. I was being ridiculous.

I tentatively shared this experience with my older sister who made a simple statement that changed the trajectory of my thoughts and ultimately gave me the language to locate myself in the midst of a chaotic period of time. Christy said, "My counselor told me that it would probably take at least two years just to get over the initial trauma of this summer's events."

I bristled at that word "trauma." Trauma was a word that belonged to other people. It was a word to describe horrific car accidents or sexual assault. "Traumatic" was the word I used to describe the experiences of the college women that gathered in my house on Sunday evenings to find solidarity with other survivors of sexual abuse. They could claim the term, not me. It seemed melodramatic to label the events leading up to my hate mail as being "traumatic."

But that word got me thinking. I thought of the "triggers" the Sunday night women shared: basements and doorknobs and lines from songs. And I began to wonder if the sound of the mail truck was a trigger for me. I gradually became aware of other triggers that had crept into my life that summer—one in particular that was especially painful.

I've journaled since I was a child—regularly, religiously. That summer prompted an unforeseen series of events resulting in memories drawn from my childhood journals being shared in a public, ecclesial setting. The words I shared in confidence for a private intervention were shared publicly. My multiple requests for confidentiality and privacy went unheeded. I remember learning my trust had been breached and sitting perfectly still in my family room while it got later and later at night. I sat there for a long time in that room, watching it change from dusk to dark feeling violated, powerless, and exposed as my words disseminated into public space.

I stopped journaling. After two decades of keeping journals, I was done. It was not a conscious decision, but the desire to write was simply gone. Even the *thought* of a journal made me literally sick to my stomach.[2] I packed up the old journals I kept on a bookshelf in my bedroom and relegated them to a closet.

Did events like these constitute trauma? Could I legitimately claim mail trucks and journals as triggers? Partway through that summer I decided to experiment. Despite the embarrassment I felt in claiming such a serious moniker for my experiences, I decided that for the remainder of the summer, I was going to treat what happened to me as *traumatic*. "Trauma" would be a part of my autobiographical articulation—at least for the summer. I wouldn't try to evaluate *where* my experience landed on the pain scale—I would simply accept it as "trauma" and see where that led.

It led to Serene Jones. I can scarcely describe the validation I felt while reading *Trauma and Grace: Theology in a Ruptured World* at my kitchen table.[3] Phrases like "beyond one's ability to cope" and "fractured imagination" helped me to identify and name my experiences more accurately. Jones served as my literary tour guide through the murky world of trauma I had been blindly navigating. To say I am grateful for her work would be a vast understatement.

Soon after reading Jones, my mentor and friend, Kenda, called simply to see how I was coping. My answer was "Not well," and I attempted to articulate the painful events in fragments and stutters. Kenda listened. She paused. And then she said: "It sounds like Jesus is asleep on your boat." In that simple phrase, Kenda gave me an image of God that I could live with. I had not been sure of what to do with God up until this point. Everyone involved in the scandal was claiming a corner market on God. Either we were playing a Christological tug-of-war with a clear winner and loser, or else God was contradicting God's self over and over again. Was God mine? Was God theirs? The real elephant in the room, however, was my unarticulated fear that this God I had given my life to was no more than a religious placebo pill.

I didn't have to declare God a figment of my imagination, nor did I have to label God a villain. God was here. God was with me. But God was asleep on the boat with his head on a cushion, which meant any anger I felt toward God seemed justified. I wasn't even close to tackling questions of theodicy, and so Kenda constructed a theological space—a divine waiting room where I could put my faith. I'm convinced Kenda is a major factor in why I didn't walk away from the church that summer.

It was around this time John and I celebrated our eleventh anniversary. We went out for pizza and then walked the grounds of a nearby monastery—a far cry from jetted tubs and roses. I had been reluctant to leave my kids at home that day. I'd found they grounded me and kept me in the present like nothing else. They required just enough of me that I could be briefly distracted from my problems. Their chaos was all consuming and strangely comforting. You could say I overmedicated on preschoolers. It was my anniversary, however, and so I convinced myself booking a sitter was a wise move and off we went.

In the back of the monastery was a large labyrinth. I had always been secretly bored by labyrinths. They were always too long. Always too slow. They didn't lead anywhere. This particular labyrinth wasn't impressive. In the center of the labyrinth was a large, dead tree. I imagine at one point it was a beautiful sight and offered shade to pilgrims. Now, however, it was just a jagged stump shooting up about 5 feet into the air.

John sat and read while I began the walk. For the first time, I was grateful for the long, slow road in front of me. The path was marked with rocks so I didn't have to think about where I was going. I could walk on autopilot. I was so tired of thinking—more specifically, tired of thinking about *myself*. The mental quiet was a gift. I was startled when I arrived at the center of the labyrinth with a relatively clear head and a startling realization. When I returned to John I remarked, "I don't want justice. I don't even know what justice would look like in these circumstances. I want beauty. Something that transcends all of this that I can lose myself in."

There was something satisfying in being able to identify something that I wanted, and while I don't remember much of what I did that summer (or that whole year, actually), I know that I painted. I painted a lot. Our dining room chairs were all different colors that summer—coral one day and green the next. I painted maps of New Jersey, a state that had unexpectedly burrowed its way into my heart and symbolized a home that still felt safe. I broke our neighborhood association rules and painted our front door a bright yellow. John joked that every time he walked into our house it was different than when he had left. Beauty and pain were my trailheads that summer, and they have continued to be so.

This book is my attempt to integrate trauma and the lived church experience. Obviously, this is not a novel attempt—Jones along with many others has taken on this project in deep and thorough ways I will not attempt to recreate here. What I am hoping to contribute to this burgeoning field, however, is the inclusion of testimony, more specifically articulation theory to the conversation.

A few years ago, I wrote a book on testimony and spiritual formation.[4] The book addresses how the act of testifying within a particular community helps form our spiritual identities. We modify, correct, and strengthen our beliefs in ongoing relationships with significant others. We maintain our identities oftentimes through our conversations with others. When I testify, I am not only describing an event of the past but also constructing my present identity through articulation. What's more, my witness affects not only myself but also those around me. Within that first book I developed a "Theory of Articulation" as an attempt to describe what I've shared in figure 1.1.[5]

My experiences with the mail truck and the journal left me wondering what a theory of articulation would have to say about trauma. Could testimony play a role in constructing a cohesive narrative identity in the wake of trauma? This book pushes many of these elements further. Where my earlier work focuses on the effect of articulating one's story as far as their faith is concerned, this book focuses more on the relationships in those liminal spaces *between* event, articulation, and recognition, particularly as it relates to trauma. You might say this book is the theory of that first book simply played in a different key.

When we encounter a traumatic event, if we are able to find space to articulate that trauma and if our trauma is appropriately recognized, we are able to

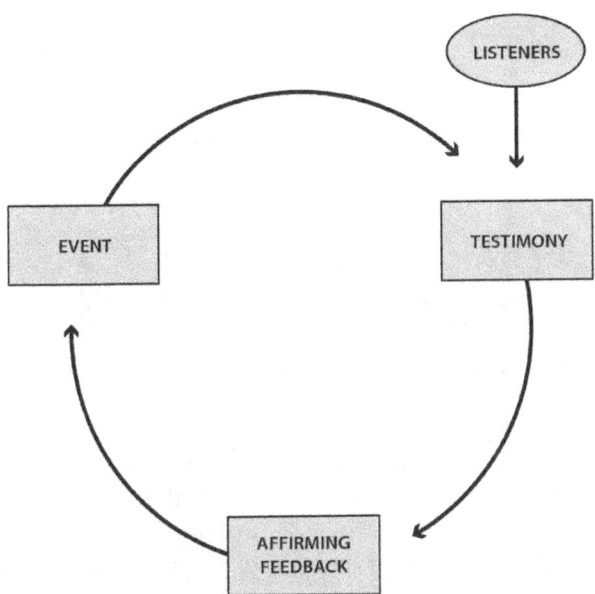

Figure 1.1 Articulacy Loop with Listeners. *Source*: From *Saying is Believing* by Amanda Hontz Drury. Copyright (c) 2015 by Amanda Hontz Drury. Used by permission of InterVarsity Press, P. O. Box 1400, Downers Grove, IL 60515. www.ivpress.com.

better integrate pain into the narratives of our lives. The inability to integrate traumatic experiences into our lives is what makes trauma particularly disorienting. Theologian Shelly Rambo puts it this way: "Suffering is what, in time, can be integrated into one's understanding of the world. Trauma is what is not integrated in time; it is the difference between a closed and an open wound."[6] Simply put, trauma is suffering that is not integrated into our lives. Those who have seen the Pixar film, *Inside Out* may recall the memory marbles categorized and stored within Riley's brain. Drawing upon that image, trauma is the loose marble rolling around in our brains without a proper home. Various forms of trauma therapy seek to reintegrate the traumatic moments through various methods. Put more succinctly, trauma therapy strives to keep us from losing our marbles.

We need others in order to help put the marbles back in place. My hope is that this book might help illustrate what it looks like for the Body of Christ to recognize trauma. I don't mean recognition in the "I see it and identify it" kind of way—certainly the church recognizes trauma in that sense regularly. The kind of recognition I am pursuing is a deep mutual recognition not *of* the other but *with* the other. It is more than seeing or empathizing. Indeed, our very personhood is wrapped up in recognition of the other. I am operating within a Hegelian understanding that the formation of our

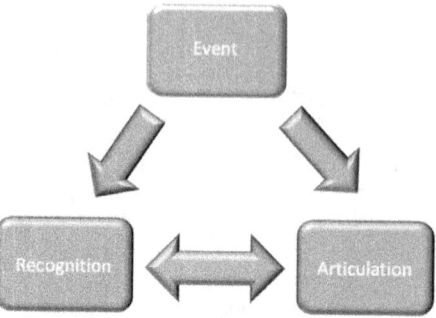

Figure 1.2 Recognition within the Articulacy Loop.

identities and the way in which we categorize these identities and memories involves a kind of dialogical relationship of mutual recognition with the other. Frederick Beiser writes: "Hegel contends that the self knows itself to be a rational being only if it recognizes the equal and independent reality of others, and only if the others recognize its own equal and independent reality"[7] (see figure 1.2).

This kind of recognition of the traumatized, however, does more than validate and affirm the other. This recognition also shapes our own identities. And if this kind of recognition is not experienced, our suffering is compounded.

"Our identity," Charles Taylor writes,

> is partly shaped by recognition or its absence, often by the misrecognition of others, and so a person or group of people can suffer real damage, real distortion, if the people or society around them mirror back to them a confining or demeaning or contemptible picture of themselves. Nonrecognition or misrecognition can inflict harm, can be a form of oppression, imprisoning someone in a false, distorted, and reduced mode of being.[8]

The philosopher Robert Williams clarifies: "Recognition culminates, not in a logic of oppression or repression, but in a reciprocal relationship between such alternatives."[9] Williams continues by quoting *Hegel's Early Theological Writings*: "To conceive is to dominate . . . but only in love one is at-one with the object, neither dominating it nor dominated by it."[10] In short, recognition means freedom in its broadest sense.

The remainder of this book is an exploration of the dialogical relationship between articulation and recognition as it relates to traumatic events. As is often the case, it is most helpful to explore abstract concepts within the confines of real life. The language of trauma and how it is understood within society gives us a common ground on which to begin. Many of the stories I share in this book are difficult. They are not your average, everyday experiences. It is the excessive trauma within these stories that highlight the commonalities of the traumas we more regularly encounter. As Kierkegaard explains, "The exception explains the general as well as itself. And when one really wants to study the general, one need only look around for a real exception."[11] It should be noted that for the most part, these stories focus less on the traumatic event and more on what *follows* the traumatic event—namely, in the articulation and recognition of these events. While the events themselves are not overly detailed, they are named as honestly as possible.

Sometimes when we are exposed to stories of trauma we border on sadistic voyeurism leaving some to question the value of trauma narratives. Nevertheless, these are important stories to tell. The Italian philosopher Giorgio Agamben writes of the necessity of speaking of evil. Speaking of Auschwitz, he writes that to say something

> is "unsayable" or "incomprehensible" is equivalent to *euphemein*, to adoring in silence, as one does with a god. Regardless of one's intentions, this contributes to its glory. We, however, "are not ashamed of staring into the unsayable"—even at the risk of discovering that what evil knows itself, we can also find in ourselves.")[12]

So, we speak, we testify, and we recognize the testimony of others. And in so doing we often find our narratives intermingling with others in surprising ways, often leading us to greater recognition of the other and the self.

"Hyperlink Cinema" is a term used in Hollywood to describe those movies that begin with multiple stories that appear to be standalone plots which eventually merge into one big story.[13] The random characters at the beginning end up having some kind of connection to one another. It's a genre of interlocking narratives or intertwining stories. In some ways, the stories that emerge in this book have a "hyperlink" element to them where over the course of four years, a horse accident, a sudden death, and an assault bring together three women, intertwining their stories in such a way that they almost can't tell their own stories without referencing the others.

I am beyond grateful for the women that spent many hours with me, answering my questions and allowing their stories to be recorded. These are three distinct stories of three distinct individuals drawn together under the umbrella of trauma. While all of the women have graciously agreed to share their stories, minor edits have been made to respect their privacy.

These stories intermingle with trauma research, articulation theory, and theological interludes in order to name traumatic events, articulate the existence and influence of trauma, and subsequently explore how the church body might recognize trauma.

The chapters in this book proceed as follows:

Chapter 1: Testimony and Trauma This chapter contains a general overview of the whole book drawing from stories and experiences of ten college women who are all survivors of sexual abuse. In it we see relationships emerge between event, articulation, and recognition on a macro level—this is the mountaintop view of the arguments within this book. The subsequent chapters break down these elements on a more micro level.

Chapter 2: Event: When Trauma Takes Over This chapter focuses on a young mother named Sarah whose six-year-old son, Jacob, experiences a serious head injury.[14] The traumatic event he experiences is almost a textbook case study of the common, yet frightening, elements of post-traumatic stress disorder. Many of the concepts and descriptions provided within this chapter echo what is currently seen in trauma literature. Jacob's mother, Sarah, met with me multiple times to describe their family's experience of encountering trauma.

Chapter 3: Articulation: Speaking the Unspeakable Here we focus on the role of articulation in traumatic events and the struggle to put words to our experiences. Within this chapter, we read Karen's struggle to articulate the sudden loss of her husband in a backyard accident. Karen beautifully describes the difficulty in knowing what to share, how to share, and where to share it—particularly in light of faith convictions of triumphal joy and life. Karen's experience specifically identifies the challenges professing Christians face in knowing how to speak of trauma.

Chapter 4: Recognition This chapter follows the story of a young mother who encounters a violent assault within her own home as well as the healing manner in which she is recognized by her community. It is, perhaps, the best example I've found of properly recognized trauma. Her story is horrific but contains deep and beautiful threads of hope. This chapter will help deepen our understanding of recognition and will nuance our understanding with feminist critiques of recognition and redistribution. She would tell you that her story is a testimony to hope.

Between each of these chapters theological interludes have been inserted, seeking to add an additional theological depth from another voice.

CLARIFYING THE CONCEPTS: EVENTS

Before delving into the chapters to come, I'd like to pause and clarify some of the terminologies used within this articulacy theory. When I speak of "events" I am meaning traumatic events. Chapters 2 and 3 highlight many of the characteristics of traumatic events. The descriptions of trauma given here are not new—they are a reflection of what is often seen in trauma literature. Those familiar with the world of trauma literature will recognize many of the facts and descriptions provided.

My definition of a traumatic event is taken from leading clinical psychologists who refer to these events as *"one in which a person or persons perceives themselves or others as threatened by an external force that seeks to annihilate them and against which they are unable to resist and which overwhelms their capacity to cope."*[15] It is important to emphasize that this occurs if the person believes that an external force is threatening them. It does not matter if in fact they are safe; if they *perceive* this threat as dangerous it is considered traumatic.[16]

Not long ago I picked up my six-year-old daughter from kindergarten and noticed something seemed off. Clara was very quiet on the ride home, and my normally cheerful little girl was quick to cry for the remainder of the day. Our questions didn't yield answers, and while she was quick to accept snuggles, we were nevertheless at a loss over what was bothering her. I put her to bed hoping for some kind of a "reset button" in the night; however, when she awoke the next morning her tears were still quick to fall. None of her reactions made sense until we were about three minutes from her school. As I made the turn onto the street near Clara's school she quietly asked, "Do people die if they eat paper?"

Knowing where this conversation was going I quickly responded, "No, Honey, people don't die from eating paper." Pause. "Clara, did you eat paper?"

The tears began to fall once again as Clara explained how she had eaten the corner of a piece of paper and her friend had told her that now she was going to die. Clara had spent the last fifteen hours concerned that she had a ticking time bomb in her stomach. After reassuring her that she would in fact survive, she bounded from the car and returned home that day as a light-hearted child. Clara's life was never in danger. At no point was it even threatened. But she perceived herself to be in a dangerous position, hence the fear and the crying. This is perhaps a silly example; however, it highlights how the power of perception makes the bearer of the experience the determining factor in whether or not the experience was traumatic.

CLARIFYING THE CONCEPTS: ARTICULATION

The kind of articulation I speak of is the sometimes near-impossible task of finding words to describe traumatic events. Articulating trauma is more difficult than it may sound. Agamben speaks of the tendency to either claim to fully understand an articulation or to avoid any kind of understanding at all, offering instead "only cheap mystifications."[17] In many ways testimony is grossly inadequate, particularly so far as trauma is concerned. Even if I testify to a traumatizing experience in a moment-by-moment format complete with video footage, my words are nonetheless inadequate.

Someone might understand or empathize, but they cannot completely experience what it is I have experienced. Agamben identifies an "essential lacuna" that exists within testimony where "survivors bore witness to something it is impossible to bear witness to."[18] The way forward, he claims, is in paying attention to this lacuna that exists between a confident understanding and a "cheap mystification." We listen to the silence. We take in the words uttered and attempt to listen to that which is silent as well. This is not simple. Agamben admits, "Listening to something absent did not prove fruitful for this author."[19] This lacuna creates space for shame to emerge: I have had a traumatic experience. I cannot adequately speak to that experience. I cannot justify my present condition by explaining my past—they do not add up. And suddenly the trauma is compounded with shame.

The words we use to describe our lives are always inadequate—they are lacking before we begin. While this inadequacy shouldn't silence our voices, it should prompt us to proceed with humility. Judith Butler explains:

> We can surely still tell our stories, and there will be many reasons to do precisely that. But we will not be able to be very authoritative when we try to give a full account with a narrative structure. The "I" can tell neither the story of its own emergence nor the conditions of its own possibility without bearing witness to a state of affairs to which one could not have been present, which are prior to one's own emergence as a subject who can know, and so constitute a set of origins that one can narrate only at the expense of authoritative knowledge.[20]

It is impossible to give a complete and accurate account of one's own story—regardless of whether or not trauma is present. Judith Butler speaks of a personal narrative as a "story that arrives belatedly, missing some of the constitutive beginnings and the preconditions of the life it seeks to narrate."[21] She explains: "I cannot be present to a temporality that precedes my own capacity for self-reflection."[22]

This is more than simply saying I am the product of my environment. There are forces and factors at work prior to my own consciousness that I am neither privy to nor could articulate even if I tried. Butler explains that our narratives always begin in the middle of the story.[23] "I am always recuperating, reconstructing, and I am left to fictionalize and fabricate origins I cannot know."[24] Regardless of how articulate or eloquent one is, "my account of myself is partial, haunted by that for which I can devise no definitive story.

I cannot explain exactly why I have emerged in this way, and my efforts at narrative reconstruction are always undergoing revision. There is that in me and of me for which I can give no account."[25]

In some ways, our awareness of this inability to fully narrate our stories deeply connects us to others. An awareness of this kind constitutes "a disposition of humility and generosity . . . I will need to be forgiven for what I cannot have fully known and I will be under a similar obligation to offer forgiveness to others who are also constituted in partial opacity to themselves."[26] This cultivates within us a kind of patience that suspends "the demand that they be self-same at every moment."[27] This is of particular importance given current emphases placed on authenticity. Furthermore, Butler writes, "Suspending the demand for self-identity or, more particularly, for complete coherence seems to me to counter a certain ethical violence, which demands that we manifest and maintain self-identity at all times and requires others to do the same."[28]

Butler explains at length how this kind of humility, generosity, and patience cultivates a fitting spirit of recognition for the other:

> As we ask to know the other, or ask that the other say, finally or definitively, who he or she is, it will be important not to expect an answer that will ever satisfy. By not pursuing satisfaction and by letting the question remain open, even enduring, we let the other live, since life might be understood as precisely that which exceeds any account we may try to give of it.[29]

Perhaps this is the simplest definition of recognition: allowing this unknown part to simply "live."

While our self-narration is insufficient and incomplete, it nevertheless is indelibly linked to how we understand ourselves and our identities. There is a rich philosophical tradition linking narrative to identity. We talk ourselves into who we are. Speaking of adolescents, Charles Taylor claims we are able to engage in our most authentic selves when we are given the space to articulate who we are. Our words create, modify, clarify, and strengthen our understandings of self.[30] Our words are powerful. And so, when we have an experience we cannot articulate, our identities take a blow. How do we articulate something that words cannot adequately capture?

Of course, articulation alone does not solidify an identity. However, the recognition one receives in response to their words has a profound effect on one's sense of self. When I speak of an experience I am not only describing something that happened in the past but also constructing my understanding of my present self. Articulating who we are is always limited, but even more so when we attempt to speak of trauma, particularly because trauma often results in the inability to offer a coherent, flowing narrative.

It is here we see how the transcendent nature of speaking of trauma is echoed in the impossibility of speaking of a transcendent God. Both the desolation and consolation leave us speechless, yet both seem to require some kind of articulation. This is despite the fact that such a task is impossible, and we have, in a sense, failed before we've even begun.[31]

CLARIFYING THE CONCEPTS: RECOGNITION

Throughout this book I draw from four different forms of recognition, or in many cases, forms of *mis*-recognition which have been considerably simplified below:

1. *Recognition*: The first form of recognition is quite simple—I recognize an old friend walking along the street and I greet her by name: "Hello, Rosa."
2. *Misrecognition*: Then again, let's say I see Rosa on the street. I know that she is familiar to me; however, I wrongfully come to the conclusion that this is Janet from my daughter's carpool lane. Here I have misrecognized Rosa.
3. *Unrecognition*: Perhaps, however, my friend looks quite different from the last time that I saw her. She now has glasses; her hair is a different color and she has lost some weight. I see this woman walking toward me on the street, but I do not recognize her as someone I know. She is in front of me yet she is unrecognizable.
4. *Nonrecognition*: Or perhaps I see Rosa on the street but for whatever reason I do not acknowledge her. I increase my gait and refrain from even making eye contact with her. She is now, to me, nonrecognized.

Or consider a fictional account of two men in two distinct places—let's call them David and Jamar. Both are robbed in the same evening, by the same perpetrators, in the same manner, and have had stolen from them the same items. David recounts the story of the robbery to a friend and is met with horrified gasps, empathetic utterings, and inquiries of concern. David's story is recognized in a seemingly appropriate manner that will hopefully provide David with a sense of support and validation.

Jamar, on the other hand, gives an identical account of his experience to another friend, but instead of care and concern, Jamar is met with suspicion and interrogation: "Did you leave your door unlocked?" "Are you sure you didn't just misplace your wallet?" "Why did you drive to the police station instead of call?" The nature of this response somewhat acknowledges the burglary took place; however, this friend is not recognizing the event in a way that demonstrates love and concern for his friend. In fact, one could make the case that this friend was *mis*recognized. We will go into greater details concerning recognition and the lack of recognition in upcoming chapters.

CONCLUSION: A STORY OF RECOGNITION

In December 2014 I became enamored with a painting. In Jacopo de Pontormo's "The Visitation." Mary and Elizabeth are at the forefront of the picture. They face each other, leaving us with only a profile. Their arms are intertwined—all elbows and shoulders. There are two additional women behind them staring straight ahead with almost expressionless faces. These two unnamed women seem to serve as silent witnesses to this reunion. They take their job very seriously, staring straight ahead in case they are someday called to testify to this moment. Far back on the left side are two men, almost completely hidden in the shadows. To this day I have no idea who they are or what they represent.

The painting is beautiful, breathtakingly so, but what arrested my attention was the facial expressions of these two women. They are not merely noticing each other; they are *gazing* at one another. It is difficult to describe other than to say you can actually *see* the deep understanding and mutual recognition the soon-to-be mothers have for one another.

I was still dealing with the aftermath of my family scandal when I encountered this painting, and though I couldn't explain why, I found myself drawn to it, looking at the image over and over again and finding solace. There was something about this scene I found incredibly moving. And as I gazed at these women gazing at each other I felt known. The expressions on their faces awakened me to a desire for whatever it was those two women had. I wanted to be seen in that way. To be gotten, if you will. I gazed at this picture, and it gazed at me in return.

I came across this picture when I was hungry for meaningful women mentors in my life. I had come to the surprising realization that the vast majority of my mentors had been men and so I began a quest of intentionally fostering relationships with older women. I deeply desired the kind of recognition I saw between those two women. It was so intimate that I was convinced I was missing out on something if I could not have that same recognition with another. It was fascinating to me that I could feel so understood by a 500-year-old painting. Knowing I loved this painting, my husband bought me a print for my thirty-fourth birthday. It is hanging on a wall in my office. I see it regularly, and each time I am filled with gratitude and longing.

A year went by before I began to see the picture differently. A teenager bounded into my office this past summer and stopped suddenly when she saw the print. I briefly explained to her my appreciation for the women's expressions. She listened then announced as if it were slowing dawning on her: "I know that picture! We studied it in high school." At the time, I knew next to nothing about the picture, oddly enough I didn't even know the artist's name, and so I was eager to hear Lexi's thoughts.

Lexi talked to me about this transitionary moment in the art world and how the artist's decision to use vibrant colors was unusual for the time. She pointed out the perspective of the picture and how the figures appeared to be floating—something I had noticed before but hadn't really *see*. Her words enhanced my understanding of the painting. I still saw that mutual recognition, but I was also aware of the hand and mind of the rebellious painter which made me like it even more.

Now, upon hearing about my relationship with this picture Lexi could have responded in a number of ways. She could have said something like, "You say you love this painting, but you can't even name the artist?" She could have lorded her knowledge over me while speaking in a condescending manner. She also could have completely ignored the Pontormo on the wall. Instead, she recognized the painting, and she recognized me. What took place in my office that summer was a mutual recognition between Lexi and myself. We sat there in mutual recognition, staring at the painting of two women engaging in their own kind of mutual recognition.

This story in the form of a theory of articulation would look something like this:

1. *Event*: Lexi walks into my office and encounters the painting.
2. *Articulation*: I share with Lexi why this painting has so much meaning to me.
3. *Recognition*: Lexi receives my words and engages in deep conversation based on what I shared.

And now, my entire encounter with Lexi is wrapped up in a single experience. When I go home from my office on that particular day and tell my husband, John, about the invigorating conversation with Lexi, he recognizes the significance of this encounter and shares in my joyful delight.

1. *Event*: Lexi and I experience a mutual recognition upon encountering this picture.
2. *Articulation*: I tell John about this encounter with Lexi.
3. *Recognition*: John rejoices with me.

My interaction with Lexi does more than simply increase my knowledge of the picture. It enhanced my relationship with Lexi and sparked within me a hunger to know more about the picture. And so even though I'd had the painting for a year-and-a-half, it wasn't until my encounter with Lexi that I started researching the painting.

In my research, I came across a short documentary on the 2014 restoration of Pontormo's "Visitation." And suddenly the picture took on even more meaning. The greens and pinks I saw were actually reds and blues when properly restored. The dark shadowy figures in the back actually had more life to them than I had originally thought. And apparently, somewhere in the picture is a donkey's head poking out from behind a building, though it's not present in the print on my office wall.

The point is this: I've always been looking at the same painting, but every time I've interacted with the picture, my understanding of it has changed. I keep coming back to the same painting but with a richer and more complete understanding of what it is. And even though my print does not do justice to the newly restored original in the small city of Carmignano, I can still see the hints of blues and reds behind the faded colors on the print in my office. I return to the painting over and over again, and each time I've done so, I've interacted with it differently. There are layers of interpretation within these moments of mutual recognition, and as a result, I am different.

NOTES

1. In the years that it's taken to write this book I have debated how much of my own story to tell. I've written, deleted, written, and deleted again. Ultimately, I've decided to keep this part of my story intentionally vague. In some ways that may seem unfair, especially since I'm delving so deeply into the painful stories of others. These stories, however, involve many people that I care about. And while they have graciously given me permission to share, I am nevertheless choosing instead simply to talk about how this experience has affected me.

2. This connection between body and soul is attested to not only in trauma literature, but in theological studies as well. Karl Barth speaks to the inseparability of body and soul: "The soul of [their] body—wholly and simultaneously both, in ineffaceable difference, inseparable unity, and indestructible order." Karl Barth, *Church Dogmatics III.2 The Doctrine of Creation* (London: T & T Clark, 2009), 119.

3. Serene Jones, *Trauma and Grace: Theology in a Ruptured World* (Louisville, KY: Westminster John Knox Press, 2009).

4. Amanda Drury, *Saying is Believing: The Necessity of Testimony in Adolescent Spiritual Formation* (Chicago: InterVarsity Press, 2015).

5. Drury, *Saying is Believing*, 77.

6. Shelly Rambo, *Spirit and Trauma: A Theology of Remaining* (Louisville: Westminster John Knox Press, 2010), 7. In a dissertation dating back to 1688 from the University of Basel, Johannes Hofer wrote about trauma calling it the "disordered imagination, whereby the part of the brain chiefly affected is that part

in which the images are located." Jones writes: "Although we have more sophisticated language to describe the workings of the brain today, Hofer's insight is still remarkably accurate with respect to what we know about trauma. A traumatic event reconfigures the imagination, affecting our ability to tell stories about ourselves and our world that are life giving and lead to our flourishing." Jones, *Trauma and Grace*, 20.

7. "Hegel combines realism with an emphasis on the social dimension of knowledge . . . but for Hegel, intersubjectivity is not a replacement for realism but its very foundation. What Hegel essentially does in these chapters is to socialize Kant's idealism so that the 'I' of Kant's 'I think' must be part of a 'we think.'" Frederick Beiser, *Hegel* (New York: Routledge 2005), 177–78.

This argument has prompted some important critiques concerning whether or not our identities require another. See Nancy Fraser, "Social Justice in the Age of Identity Politics: Redistribution, Recognition, and Participation," in *Redistribution or Recognition? A Political-Philosophical Exchange*, ed., Nancy Fraser and Axel Honneth (New York: Verso, 2003) 7–119. And Elizabeth Grosz, *Becoming Undone: Darwinian Reflections on Life, Politics and Art* (Durham, NC: Duke University Press, 2011).

8. Charles Taylor, *Multiculturalism: Examining the Politics of Recognition* (Princeton University Press: Princeton NJ, 2011), 25.

9. Robert R. Williams, *Hegel's Ethics of Recognition* (Berkeley: University of California Press, 2000), 67.

10. Williams, *Hegel's Ethics of Recognition*, 67–68. Williams is drawing from Hegel's Entwürfe *über Religion und Liebe*, Theorie-Werkausgabe (1797–1798), 1:246.

11. Giorgio Agamben, *Remnants of Auschwitz: The Witness and the Archive* (New York: Zone Books, 1999), 48.

12. Agamben, *Remnants*, 33.

13. This genre is a term coined by the film critic Alissa Quart in "Hyperlink Cinema and the Presence of Intertwining Stories," *The Artiface*, 2017. Accessed October 16, 2017, https://the-artifice.com/hyperlink-cinema-stories/.

14. Names have been changed for privacy.

15. Jones, *Trauma and Grace*, 13. This understanding is also found in as taken in: Bessel A. van der Kolk, *The Body Keeps Score: Integration of Mind, Brain, and Body in the Treatment of Trauma* (Phoenix, AZ: Milton H. Erickson Foundation, 2013). And Judith Lewis Herman, *Trauma and Recovery* (London: Pandora, 2015).

16. Jones, *Trauma and Grace*, 14.

17. Agamben, *Remnants*, 13.

18. Agamben, *Remnants*, 13.

19. Agamben, *Remnants*, 13.

20. Judith Butler, *Giving an Account of Oneself* (Vancouver: Crane Library at the University of British Columbia, 2011), 37. Butler continues: "When the 'I' seeks to give an account of itself, it can start with itself, but it will find that this self is already implicated in a social temporality that exceeds its own capacities for narration; indeed, when the 'I' seeks to give an account of itself, an account that must include

the conditions of its own emergence, it must, as a matter of necessity, become a social theorist." *An Account of Oneself*, 7–8.

21. Butler, *Giving an Account*, 39.
22. Butler, *Giving an Account*, 39.
23. Butler, *Giving an Account*, 39.
24. Butler, *Giving an Account*, 39.
25. Butler, *Giving an Account*, 39.
26. Butler, *Giving an Account*, 42.
27. Butler, *Giving an Account*, 41–42.
28. Butler, *Giving an Account*, 42.
29. Butler, *Giving an Account*, 42–43.
30. Charles Taylor, *Ethics of Authenticity* (Boston: Harvard University Press, 1992).
31. Speaking of Isaiah, theologian Karl Barth writes: "It is thus clear to him from the very first that what he has seen and heard demands to be expressed and proclaimed. It must go out as a human word on human lips, to be sounded forth and heard in its immeasurable positive and negative significance among all men throughout the earth. But he knows of no human mouth which is able and worthy to form and express that which corresponds to the matter. He must confess that he is a member of the community and people in which there are only unclean lips which contradict rather than correspond to the matter. He thus knows that what he has seen and heard must be expressed and yet cannot be expressed by a human mouth. It is in view of this dilemma that he cries: "Woe is me! For I am undone." Karl Barth, *Church Dogmatics* II/1 (Edinburgh: T & T Clark, 1957), 342.

Theological Interlude 1

*Christ has died. Christ has risen.
Trauma will come again.*

A case could be made that the Christian faith rests upon traumatic events. Resurrection can only take place when there's been a death. And Jesus did not die from old age. It seems like death and resurrection could create a natural space for the traumatized to reside. But just where in the Easter story do we house those suffering from trauma?

Good Friday isn't the space for the traumatized. Friday is certainly the trauma *event*, but there is a clear demarcation of these events—when they start and the finality of when they finish. Friday might represent the trauma that takes place, but it is not the space in which the traumatized can pitch their tents. Nor does Sunday, the day of resurrection, create space for the traumatized to dwell. This reasoning has led many before me to surmise that the place for the traumatized is in that space between events—Saturday. The day Jesus descends into hell seems to be a good day to carve out space for trauma. We call it "Holy Saturday" and recognize it as a liminal space between crucifixion and resurrection; it's the space between life and death. While the events of Good Friday have come to an end, the shame and trauma of the public execution still hang heavy and quiet on Saturday. In this section, we will look at the power of this Holy Saturday imagery as well as its limitations with the ultimate hope of living into the fullness of the Paschal Mystery.

Walter Brueggemann fears the church has not properly acknowledged this liminal space.[1] We must continue our declaration of a risen Lord; however, "the second day looms larger, deeper, and more seriously than we had noticed in the drama we Christians regularly confess and claim. The rush to the third day must be profoundly slowed," he writes.[2] Brueggemann points out how quiet the church has been concerning Holy Saturday. "It is to be noticed," he writes, and for our purposes important, that the church has had very little to say about the "second day," so that in effect the drama is reduced to a two-day sequence. The two-day accent is evident in the kerygma of 1 Corinthians 15:3-6 that has no comment on the "second day" and in the contemporary widely shared formula: Christ has died, Christ is risen, Christ will come again.[3]

Theologian Shelly Rambo beautifully describes Holy Saturday as "the middle":

> [T]he middle speaks to the perplexing space of survival. It is a largely untheologized site, because the middle is overshadowed by the other two events. Because of its precarious positioning, the middle can easily be covered over and ignored. . . . The good news of Christianity for those who experience trauma rests in the capacity to theologize this middle. It does not rest in either the event of the cross or the resurrection, but instead in the movements between the two.[4]

In her theologizing of "the middle," Rambo carves out space for unresolved trauma to linger. Holy Saturday provides a place where the traumatized can find solidarity with others knowing they wait in their pain with saints and disciples of the past. Holy Saturday gently nudges both Friday and Sunday to create more space on the bench. It reassures us there is a place for us to reside that is neither death nor life. It gives us permission to lament. "You belong here," Saturday says to the individual who is no longer sure whether she is dead or alive.

LIMITATIONS WITH HOLY SATURDAY

When we see our sisters and brothers in this space, we desire to take pain seriously without rushing to the resurrection. We strive to be present to the devastation without trying to tidy anything up. We run from false platitudes: "It was God's will," "He's in a better place," or "God won't give you more than you can handle," all phrases that are meant to move us forward, to push us (sometimes violently) into resurrection.[5]

And yet those of us who profess Jesus Christ believe that this day of devastation is not a passive day. This is not merely a waiting room for the traumatized until healing begins to emerge. Rather, we believe there is movement even if it's unseen. Jesus Christ has descended into hell and is stomping out death with death. And I do not have to see or sense or even believe that's taking place in order for it to be true. I am not required to have a plan to heal from trauma in order to have hope. Hope is not reserved for those who are whole or even see themselves on the path to wholeness. If we lament, we have hope.

There are other challenges in claiming Holy Saturday for the traumatized. The fear is that a trauma survivor either (a) believes she is unable to experience the risen God of Easter until she has successfully healed from her Saturday trauma or (b) experiences the risen God, only to be crushed by the realization that Easter has occurred but her trauma remains. Certainly, greater nuance is needed.

The first challenge assumes the position that I cannot be with the risen Lord until I am whole. Jesus Christ is not the antidote but the reward. Let all those other people proceed into Sunday, I will remain in my anxious striving until I find healing. The great danger of this position is that sometimes the "fractured imagination" of the hopeless leads us to Judas's Field of Blood.

The second challenge provides its own kind of devastation when an individual encounters Jesus and later finds trauma once again rearing its head. "I have seen the risen Lord and I am still a mess." Either Jesus is not enough or I'm doing something wrong. This position gives way to deep-seated cynicism or crippling self-doubt.

TRAUMATIC TUESDAY

Holy Saturday is a resting spot for trauma, but trauma has not taken up permanent residence there in any linear sense of time. Trauma exists on both Friday and Saturday—and trauma abounds on the days that follow the resurrection. Rambo challenges us: "While keen attention was paid to rethinking the suffering *on the cross*, it is critical to think after the cross."[6] Yes, Jesus is alive, but the traumatic memories of Saturday creep into the space following the resurrection. The story is still one of betrayal, denial, beatings, public rejection, humiliation, and finally, execution. Experiences like this are not likely to disappear from memory. Christ has died. Christ is risen. Trauma will come again.

The events of the story and the poignant images are still seared into the minds of Jesus's followers. Clearly traumatized, Mary Magdalene cannot comprehend the Easter morning story unfolding before her eyes. She is stuck on a statement and repeats it to everyone she sees: "They have taken my Lord away . . . and I don't know where they have put him."[7] Three times Mary expresses her dismay first to Peter, then to an angel, and finally to Jesus himself.[8] Perhaps this repetition of a question and this inability to make sense of events unfolding before her eyes are evidence of trauma's reach.

Serene Jones draws from the Markean account of the women's experience at the tomb. She surmises that perhaps the abrupt, disconcerting ending of Mark's Gospel shows a way forward: "[The women] went out and fled from the tomb, for terror and amazement had seized them; and they said nothing to anyone, for they were afraid."[9] This story, she explains, which lacks a seemingly proper ending "resolves some of the tension for us while at the same time creating more."[10]

Her words are worth sharing at length:

> Mark does not offer any of the things we are waiting for. Rather, he gives us a brief and disappointing description of the women's pitiful response. They turn, in fear and astonishment, and flee. They run out of the tomb. They scatter *in silence*. Complete silence! Why? Mark answers this question for us directly, hiding nothing. They are afraid, he tells us. The Greek makes it clear that this is not the kind of theological "afraidness" that we think of as "awestruck" or "full of wonder." It is the kind of "afraidness" we usually think of as "scared"—the terror that comes after a violent, overwhelming event, a traumatic fear. They are frightened speechless. And in their terror, they fall mute and run. As they do, the Gospel message itself seems to dart away from the tomb, off down the road, and out into the space of oblivion. And then Mark stops the story.[11]

Mark's ending, she explains, "calls, not for oratory and powerful rhetoric, but for silence."[12] Jones explains that this ending is to be read as a kind of "gesture"—that Mark takes us "to the very limits of language, where we cross the threshold into silence.[13]

This same trauma that terrifies the women is what keeps the disciples huddled behind locked doors even after Easter morning has passed. "Peace be with you," Jesus declares. Yet they lock the doors while his breath is still warm on their faces. Jesus is alive! Now draw the curtains and bolt the doors. Christ has died, Christ has risen, and the disciples are terrified.

A week after his physical appearance, the disciples are still behind locked doors. Again, Jesus appears saying: "Peace be with you."[14] The disciples may have seen and heard that Jesus is alive, but the violence done to him is still fresh in their minds. I find it somewhat comforting to know that it's possible to be an eye witness to the resurrected God, to see the powers of death reversed, to be breathed upon by Christ himself, and to still remain huddled behind locked doors in terror.

Afterwards, John tells us, the disciples see Jesus again, this time while they are out fishing. Here, on the shores of the Sea of Tiberius, after sharing a meal, Jesus calls Simon Peter by name, reinstating and inviting him to participate in kingdom work. Peter did not earn this reinstatement. He did not jump through hoops. This wasn't something he pursued. Jesus came to Peter, not the other way around. Peter wasn't looking for Jesus; Peter was killing time by returning to an earlier vocation he had outgrown years earlier. Some might say he was regressing. But Jesus comes to the traumatized, greeting them with peace, speaking their names, and offering dignity. And he does so with scars clearly marked on his hands.

Trauma emerges well after death itself has been ruptured. Following the ascension, as Jesus's followers are trying to figure out what this new life looks like, we see it continue to unfold. I wonder what was more traumatic: watching the first Christian martyr stoned before their eyes, or realizing three days later that Stephen really wasn't coming back. We have beatings, imprisonment, the shame of being run out of town, and the indignity of allowing friends to lower you in baskets. Fresh wounds are seen in Paul's writing to the Corinthians. He writes of affliction that left them "so utterly, unbearably crushed that we despaired of life itself. Indeed, we felt that we had received the sentence of death."[15] And Peter's first epistle is written for the traumatized—those displaced by persecution who are scattered across the land.[16]

All of this leads us to the question: what does it look like to experience trauma alongside the risen Lord?[17] What does Holy Saturday mean in light of the resurrection? Holy Saturday is a testament to there being space for the traumatized. Holy Saturday is a testament to a journey; it is not a destination. We live with Easter behind us as well as Easter before us. We come after Christ's resurrection, yet we are before our own. This too is a liminal space between life and death. In some ways, one might argue our entire existence is its own kind of Holy Saturday, existing between death and resurrection.

Experiencing trauma alongside the risen Lord means we acknowledge there are many different ways of encountering Jesus. John describes various experiences of individuals encountering Jesus, but he does not prescribe these experiences. Some recognize Jesus, some do not. Some are actively looking, others are not. Some meet Jesus in open fields, others behind locked doors. To each one Jesus speaks words of peace.

Experiencing trauma alongside the risen Lord means walking alongside a God who is scarred. Jesus emerges from the tomb with a testimony of trauma engraved on his hands, feet, and side. Speaking of these wounds, Rambo writes: "The resurrection scars suggest that we will need to find ways to speak about how the wounds of others form us, not solely to mark us for death but also to mark us for life."[18]

These scars are not romanticized; rather they are a testament of God with us. Even in his glory he identifies with us, drawing our attention to his scars—those imperfections that demonstrate solidarity.

NOTES

1. This attention to Holy Saturday is certainly not new nor exclusive to Brueggemann as we clearly see in the writings of Hans urs von Balthasar, Alan Lewis, Serene Jones, Rowan Williams, Cornell West, Shelly Rambo, etc.

2. Walter Brueggemann, "Reading From the Day 'In Between.'" In *A Shadow of Glory: Reading the New Testament After the Holocaust*, edited by Tod Linafelt (New York: Routledge, 2002), 111. Drawing upon the work of philosopher George Steiner, Brueggemann explains how the world—both Christians and non-Christians alike—is aware of the significance of both Good Friday and Easter Sunday. "But," he writes quoting Steiner, "ours is the long day's journey of the Saturday. Between suffering, aloneness, unutterable waste on the one hand and the drama of liberation, of rebirth on the other. In the face of the torture of a child, of the death of love which is Friday, even the greatest art and poetry are almost helpless." Brueggemann, "In Between," 112.

3. Brueggemann, "In Between," 108.

4. Shelly Rambo, *Spirit and Trauma: A Theology of Remaining* (Louisville: Westminster John Knox Press, 2010), 7–8. Throughout this section I will be in continual conversation both with Rambo and with Serene Jones. I am deeply appreciative of the ways in which they have shaped the churches understanding of trauma and the Paschal Mystery. Within this conversation I will pose some critical questions in order that we might live even more into the fullness of the Paschal Mystery.

5. See Kate Bowler, *Everything Happens for a Reason and Other Lies I've Loved* (New York: Random House, 2018).

6. Shelly Rambo, *Resurrecting Wounds: Living in the Afterlife of Trauma* (Baylor, TX: Baylor University Press, 2017), 6.

7. John 20:2; 13; 15.

8. Rowan Williams's book, *Resurrection: Interpreting the Easter Gospel*, identifies the pivotal moment in disrupting the Mary's traumatic trance of searching for the body. There is an in breaking with a simple word from Jesus: "Mary." Williams writes: "Mary is offered her name, her identity, the name which specifies her as the person with a particular story. And in this context, the utterance of the name re-establishes a relation of trust and recognition." Rowan Williams, *Resurrection: Interpreting the Easter Gospel* (London, Darton: Longman & Todd, 1982), 38–39. Mary encounters the living Lord when he appears to her and says her name, prompting her to physically take hold of him. This calling by name and physical touch seem to pull Mary solidly into the present moment. The pain of the past is present, but she is mindful to her present position in the presence of Jesus. Yes, she is instructed to not continue clinging to Jesus, and she is sent out from his presence. And yes, no doubt the memory of recent events is still raw, but she runs away with a crazy, daring hope that perhaps redemption is real.

9. Mark 16:8.

10. Jones, *Trauma*, 87.

11. Jones, *Trauma*, 89.

12. Jones, *Trauma*, 94.

13. "Why?" Jones, asks, "To show us, by means of a gesture, an embodied image of fear." His ending shows how "when sacred rhetoric meets the embedded realities of traumatic images, perhaps silence, accompanied by gesture is the only appropriate response. . . . The shadow cast by the cross becomes a dark womb that holds their brokenness and envelopes their pain. In this space there is no divine justification for

suffering, but there is the outstretched gesture of understanding, of solidarity, and of welcoming embrace." Jones, *Trauma*, 96–97.

14. John 20:26.

15. 2 Corinthians 1:8–9, NRSV

16. 1 Peter 1:6, NRSV; See Abson Joseph, *A Narratological Reading of 1 Peter* (London: T. & T. Clark, 2012).

17. Rambo argues that resurrection is "not so much about life overcoming death, as it is about *life resurrecting amid the ongoingness of death*." Rambo, Resurrecting Wounds, 7.

18. Shelly Rambo. "Resurrecting Scars" in *Feminism and Religion*. April 9, 2012.

Chapter 2

The Ten Women

So often it seems that God is found not in the cure but in the affliction. In my first-year teaching at a Christian liberal arts institution, I was asked to serve as a receiving clergy at an evening healing service. My task was to listen to the concerns of the student, pray, and anoint them with oil, making the form of the cross on their hands or foreheads. Students who desired prayer could move forward and form a line in front of one of the five clergies to await their turn.

I had seen footage of televangelists shouting flamboyant declarations of healing, and my fear was that a student would expect something similar from me. What if they came to me with a presumed definition of healing that only included a sudden, immediate miracle? Or worse, what if a student were to stop taking needed medication as "an act of faith"?

The prayer requests I heard that evening were not about cures for cancer or the mending of broken bones as I had expected. Instead, person after person approached me and said something along the lines of "I was molested as a child and I need help." "I was assaulted by a guy in high school and I can't stop thinking about it." I have a hunch that my being the only female clergy upfront predisposed certain students to choose my line over another's. That evening I listened as both women and men whispered traumatic pain they had carried around for years—all of them desiring some kind of relief. I left the chapel feeling overwhelmed and exhausted. Prior to that evening I could have quoted you the statistics on sexual assault in the United States, but there's a big difference between numbers on a page and the face of a person in front of you.

I preached in chapel soon after on the ten lepers from Luke 17. While my sermon didn't directly address trauma or abuse, there was another influx of stories directed my way—in emails, office visits, reflection papers, even random conversations in the bathroom. All of them seemed to start with, "You don't know me, but when I was 12 . . ."

It took about a month and a half of these conversations before it occurred to me that perhaps there was a need for more intentional spaces to receive these stories of pain.[1] I knew the school offered free counseling services and group workshops, but there seemed to be a hunger for something more. And so, after much prayer and counsel, another facilitator and I opened up my house for a weekly evening gathering for young women who had been sexually abused.[2]

That first Sunday I picked up my children's toys, arranged the homemade brownies, went over last-minute details with my co-facilitator, and waited, hoping that I was wrong—hoping there was not a need for this sort of thing after all. My heart sank every time I heard someone at the door that evening. Each knock represented a woman in pain. I found myself rehearsing how I would greet the women. Something seemed wrong about saying, "I'm glad you're here," so when the hesitant knocks at the front door began, we greeted the women with a simple, "Welcome" and "Thank you for coming."

That year, ten women regularly appeared on my porch on Sunday evenings.[3] We began each time with a reminder of our four guiding principles for the group: (1) all stories are confidential, (2) all stories are sacred (we will honor each story without comparing it to someone else's), (3) no one has to talk, and (4) this group was not a substitute for counseling (it was asked of the women to be engaged in therapy in addition to being a part of this group). My biggest fear was that these Sunday evenings would open up too much too soon. I was afraid of unknowingly rupturing a wound and then pushing them out my door, raw and full of pain. I'm grateful for the pastors and trauma counselors who served as advisors and sounding boards throughout this endeavor. The hope was that this group might find a space where they could share their stories and find hope, solidarity, and support from one another.

That didn't happen. Not at first, at least. Week after week that first semester our Sunday evenings were full of long, awkward pauses and darting eyes. One young woman spent every single Sunday night sitting on the floor, her back against a wall, with her hoodie pulled tightly around her face. I was convinced it was a failure.

What I didn't realize at the time was that I was attempting to create sanctioned spaces of articulation without intentional rituals of recognition in place. I thought by opening up my door people would talk. Perhaps the reason why students spoke about sexual abuse at the healing service was not only because there was sanctioned space to do so but because there were intentional rites of recognition guiding and informing their actions and articulations. They knew in advance that this particular night was designated to be a time of prayer and laying on of hands. They knew to stand in line. To wait their turn. To share their need. To pray and be anointed by oil. These rituals of recognition set certain explicit and implicit boundaries. It was clear these were going to be short conversations with clergy (though they were also given the space to not speak at all). There was no fear of a monopolization of time that would result in an hour-long conversation. By choosing their own line, students were also given the choice of receiving clergy, granting them the authority to choose to whom they spoke. They were also surrounded by dozens of other students who were engaging in these rituals of recognition. There was implicit solidarity that they were not alone in their pain. Within that simple healing service, there were established rites of recognition that carved out a safe space for articulation.

When I started the Sunday night support group I thought that recognition was my *response* to articulation. What I didn't know was that recognition is often the *invitation* for articulation. Most of the public spaces where articulation comes naturally are embedded with explicit and implicit rituals of recognition. Consider a doctor's office—even though it is expected one will likely converse with the doctor to share his concerns or questions regarding his health, he has already encountered multiple rituals of recognition along the way to pave that path to articulation. There are appointment reminder cards and phone calls. There are waiting rooms, sign-in sheets, and insurance forms. The patient is met with scales, thermometers, and stethoscopes. These are all rituals of recognition that communicate to the patient that this is an appropriate space to speak of one's health. It's rituals of recognition that signal to the patient that the doctor's office is the place for these conversations as opposed to the golf course or in line at the grocery store.[4] Recognition does not always serve as a response to articulation; in fact, recognition both precedes and follows articulation. As Kierkegaard explains: "Life can only be understood backwards; but it must be lived forwards."[5]

To speak of a traumatic event without knowing how one might be received is downright terrifying. It requires enormous fortitude on behalf of the speaker. It is going out on a limb without knowing whether or not the branch will hold or if there is someone at the bottom with a net.[6]

My internal pronouncement of Sunday night failure was quickly countered with the startling realization that despite the awkward silences, these women were still showing up week after week. They were not talking, but they were present. And so, toward the end of the first semester I initiated a conversation *about* the conversation. I asked the question: "What's it like for you to hear questions posed within this group?" I then went around the circle, inviting each woman, one at a time by name to consider the question. The women were still given an "out." They could simply say "pass" if they didn't want to say anything, but all of the women chose to speak that night anyway. Their responses sounded quite similar: "I had something I wanted to say, but I figured someone else had something more important to share." Or, "I didn't want to take up too much of the time talking about myself," and "I like it when you actually ask a question that's directed to me because then I know I'm invited to talk."

A blanket invitation to speak would not work. These particular women were looking for a clear path seeped in ritual to assure them throughout the journey that they belonged and there was space for them to speak. We decided that evening that our group needed intentional rituals of recognition, practices we could engage in that clarified boundaries and were permission-giving.[7] We began and ended in silence. In between those silences we cooked for one another. We came up with a plan of *how* we would receive the stories of those around us—week after week we focused on a different individual to share a small part of her story. Afterwards we shared a moment of silence, and then went around the circle and invited each woman by name to respond to the story with a question, a comment, or a simple, "Thank you for sharing." We ended each time together with a prayer for healing, a time of silence, and a prayer of blessing, followed by the reading of a psalm as a benediction.

What fascinated me were the organic rites of recognition these women initiated on their own. One young woman was torn between wanting to be known and wanting to remain hidden. During her first few months with the group, any time she spoke she did so with a blanket over her head. She did this with a certain element of humor and vulnerability that said, "I know this looks silly, but this is what I need to do." Another woman asked if I would be willing to leave out some of my five-year-old's toys for her to use (a request I was all too willing to fulfill). Women kneaded Play-Doh or fiddled with Legos, others brought knitting projects or mandalas to color. Within this particular group there was an ease in sharing when hands were occupied. One woman asked to leave a small stuffed animal at my house—she said there was something symbolic for her to take the stuffed animal out and put it away again when our time together was finished. While some of these rituals of recognition have remained the same throughout the years, I am always surprised at what different rituals emerge in the differing groups year after year.[8]

These rites of recognition ended up creating a space that welcomed trauma articulation. As women slowly began to share pieces of their stories, we found ourselves faced with new challenges. One of the main difficulties we sought to overcome on these Sunday nights was the temptation to compare stories—to see how my trauma compared to another. It seemed as if this sort of ranking was a coping mechanism to provide some kind of order to the chaos.

One woman addressed this head-on when she confided: "Sometimes I wish I actually had been raped instead of just molested." I was puzzled as women began to shake their heads in agreement and add their own thoughts:

"Sometimes I think it would be easier to be gang raped or something like that instead of just being date-raped." When I asked them to help me understand these sentiments, I was told that perhaps if something worse had happened, then they could justify the level of devastation they felt. There was a longing for a proper recognition of the events they had experienced and their capacity to identify what had happened to them. Perhaps a more serious event would have triggered a more serious recognition. The recognition they had received was less than affirming so perhaps the event they experienced wasn't really that significant, and they should just get over it.

I think the most meaningful part of these Sunday evenings for me was watching the women come to a greater self-recognition. Not only were these women recognizing each other in their pain, the recognition they gave the other subsequently resulted in a deeper recognition of themselves.[9] Over and over again, a woman would tell a part of her story, and almost consistently, when she came to the end, spoke of her shame and disgust that she did not do something more to stop the abuse. When asked point-blank if she felt as if she were at fault for what happened to them, every single one of the women silently raised a hand. The overall sense being, "I was abused and I am somehow at fault." This sentiment was true even for the woman who had no memories of the sexual abuse done to her as a toddler.

It was far easier for these women to exonerate their peers than themselves. It was much easier to say, "You were a child, you weren't to blame," to a friend than to themselves. The peer-to-peer exoneration and grace-giving became so prevalent on these Sunday evening times together that eventually it began to change the way they interpreted their own stories. One woman would later write:

> All I could see myself as was a slut, whore, someone who really didn't deserve any chances in life because I never stopped the abuse from happening to me. As time went by and much work [was] done, a lot of that began to disappear. Although there was still some fear . . . there was also peace in knowing that I am not alone. It's hard to believe that you are not at fault until you see how another was not at fault. You eventually begin to see yourself in their stories, and begin to understand how you, yourself could not be at fault."[10]

This woman's sentiment beautifully illustrates the dialectical relationships that began to form. Because sometimes we need to recognize our stories in others' mouths in order to recognize ourselves.[11]

Some evenings we projected our experiences upon those we loved in order to get a different understanding of our own experiences. When a woman is having difficulty mustering up grace and understanding for herself, we might ask her to identify someone who they care deeply about—perhaps a younger sister or brother. When the woman is then asked how she would respond if those acts were committed against a loved one, the simultaneous anger toward the perpetrator and tender grace toward the survivor are overwhelmingly clear. Imagining their stories on the lips of little sisters allowed these women to get a further glimpse of their own reality.

This mutual giving of grace was not limited to the contemporary stories of trauma exchanged among peers; sometimes this dialectical relationship formed between an individual and Scripture. Our group began to look at what we called "texts of trauma"[12] in order to gain a greater understanding of ourselves. It may be easier for a young woman to extend grace to Tamar than it is to receive grace for herself. This was not Tamar's fault. She was trying to take care of her brother in his illness and, "since he was stronger than she," we read, "he raped her."[13] When we are given multiple opportunities to extend grace to other survivors of trauma, we are better positioned to consider the same extension of grace to ourselves. Often times we need to hear others' stories in order to accurately hear our own.[14]

Overall, the primary role of the group was to create space for testimony as well as the subsequent recognition of both ourselves and others. It was fascinating to see how these women chose to self-disclose. Within this first group there was a strong preference for the spoken word over the written word. While there are certainly benefits for a survivor to write out her story of trauma, the women in my group came to the conclusion that at this point in their journeys it was easier to verbally articulate their stories. One woman explained: "It's one thing to say something or know something. It's another thing to put on paper and realize the concreteness this brings. It seems more real this way, scarier and more overwhelming in a lot of ways."[15] Another woman spoke of writing out parts of her story and then panicking over the physical evidence this written record left: "I did not let that journal out of my sight because I did not want anyone finding it. . . . It was a little stressful."[16]

Furthermore, I made the observation that the majority of the women in this group were honors students, and writing their trauma stories in the midst of their college careers came close to feeling like an assignment. There seemed to be less freedom to express the full sentiment of their experiences without their "inner editors" coming out to judge and edit their prose. Ultimately, these particular women did not want records; they wanted recognition.

Perhaps most important, however, was the *immediate* recognition these women received from their peers.[17] A woman could share her story and see the facial expressions of the women around her. The spoken word and the recognition were almost simultaneous. She could hear the quiet murmurs of affirmation and encouragement. She could see the compassion and concern in the other women's eyes. What's more, it is likely her own facial expressions are influencing the facial expressions of her peers. If the pain is evident on the speaker's face, it is likely evident on the faces of her listeners as well.[18] Knowing that each woman would respond to her story meant her words would not return void. And the silences became more and more bearable as they were simply wrapped up in our rituals of recognition.

Sunday evenings also became a space to test out their words—to experiment with *how* they told their stories. Near the start of the second semester a woman showed up at my door visibly shaken. She had just learned that what had happened to her was, technically speaking, considered rape—something that had not occurred to her before. She struggled with how to reinterpret her story in light of this new articulation. Although she had shared her experience with us earlier in the semester, this categorical change prompted the need to rearticulate events.

We saw how this word "rape" understandably held a great deal of power over the women. One young woman told the group how her attacker had contacted her through social media earlier that week. She told us that she informed him that she didn't want to have anything to do with him because of how their last encounter went (she preferred at that time to avoid using words like "abuse" or "rape"). Her reporting of the conversation and her subsequent processing left us heartbroken. "He said I wanted it," she said. "He told me it was consensual and I wanted it." She paused, then added quietly, "Maybe I did."

The young woman continued: "I know I told him 'no.' I know I pushed him off and ran away when the phone rang. But maybe he's right. Maybe this was something I wanted. He was so confident of that." The women tried to logically talk her out of that sentiment: "But just think, if he *did* assault you, then wouldn't it make sense that he might lie to you, too?" And, "He's just looking out for himself—he's just trying to convince himself that he's not the bad guy here."

Finally, the woman at the center of this conversation stated, "But if it was consensual then that means it was just premarital sex, and I can ask forgiveness and move on. I'd rather have premarital sex than be raped." And suddenly, the words that sounded so preposterous only moments ago made perfect sense to the group. These women were desperately trying to reclaim control over their own bodies and how they told their stories.

Much of this recognition came through finding solidarity with one another. There was an early moment of vulnerability when one woman shared how after she was raped, she then engaged in consensual sex with a number of young men in her high school. She concluded her story with, "Sometimes I feel more shame about sleeping around than I do about the rape." We observed a moment of silence, and then one by one the women began to respond:

"I slept around afterwards, too."
"I thought I was the only one."

And even the women who did not have a similar experience were eager to recognize their peers: "That makes sense to me," one woman said. "It sounds like after you were raped you wanted to do something to make it feel like you were in control of your own body again." Similar conversations occurred when a woman expressed an addiction to pornography. This had an extra layer of shame for her because "only guys struggle with that." Again, the stories she heard from the other women proved otherwise.

Perhaps the greatest moment of solidarity that first year came when discussing their mothers. None of these particular women had been sexually abused by their mothers, but the kind of recognition their mothers offered proved immensely painful. Consider the kinds of recognition the women reported below (see table 2.1):

Table 2.1   Forms of Recognition

Forms of Recognition	
Recognition	Only one of the women experienced the kind of recognition one would hope for from a mother—a kind of recognition that included actions of healing, compassion, and protection.
Misrecognition	"My mom told me, 'My brother did that to me, too. You just have to get over it.'"
	"My mom thought it was my fault for being too sexy."
Unrecognition	"My mom didn't believe me."
Nonrecognition	"My mother was right there in the room and didn't even do anything."
	"I finally got up the nerve to tell my mom and she didn't say a word. She just stood up and left, and we haven't talked about it since."

We see at least three different kinds of denial emerge in the above chart. First is the rationalization that says, "Yes, trauma has occurred, and it's your fault." Second is the minimization that comes when one acknowledges that trauma took place, but that it really isn't that big of a deal. Finally comes the simple denial that anything traumatic took place.

The lack of recognition from one as intimately connected as a mother can bring about a major internal dilemma. Who do I trust? Who do I recognize as an authoritative co-interpreter of my experience? Do I trust myself and my understanding of this experience as abuse, or do I trust my mother whom society upholds as my ideal and primary advocate? Adrienne Rich explains the dilemma:

> When we discover that someone we trusted can be trusted no longer, it forces us to reexamine the universe, to question the whole instinct and concept of trust. For a while, we are thrust back onto some bleak, jutting ledge, in a dark pierced

by sheets of fire, swept by sheets of rain, in a world before kinship, or naming, or tenderness exist; we are brought close to formlessness.[19]

If I trust my mother that perhaps this is just a normal part of life, how might that inform my relationship with the world? Is this a world in which I want to exist? If, however, I determine my mother is wrong and that I *can* trust my inner perception of trauma, then what does it mean that my own mother doesn't care enough to engage this matter with me? If my mother doesn't care, why should anyone else? Both roads, regardless of the one chosen, lead to a darker and more frightening world.

It is important to note that malrecognition from one's mother does not necessarily indicate a lack of care or love. In fact, it could be precisely out of a kind of flawed love that a mother is unwilling or unable to recognize her child's pain. Mutual recognition within trauma can be terrifying, even more so if one lacks the inner fortitude to wade through the fear and guilt and shame. The kind of recognition the daughter needs is not a one-way observation of events, but the intimacy of mutual recognition. This mutual recognition requires the mother to see where and how she may have been an agent in the events. The non-anxious presence that is so very healing in the midst of trauma may be more difficult to maintain between people that we love. A British sociologist spoke to this reality in a seminal study involving patients with schizophrenia.

In 1956 George Brown made a surprising discovery. Brown joined the Medical Research Council Social Psychiatry Unit of London and began the task of tracking newly discharged patients with schizophrenia. These long-stay patients were discharged "after they became symptomatically stable and recovered functionally."[20] Brown's work focused on factors that led to hospital readmittance. Within these observations Brown made a startling discovery:

> From the study, it was observed that the strongest link with relapse and readmission was the type of home to which patients were discharged. Surprisingly, the patients who discharged from hospital to stay with their parents or wives were more likely to get relapse and needed readmission than those who lived in lodgings or with their siblings. It was also found that patients staying with their mothers had reduced risk of relapse and readmission if patients and/or their mother went out to work. It suggested the probable adverse influence of prolonged contact of patients with their family members in influencing the degree of disability and level of functioning.[21]

In short, male patients with chronic schizophrenia did better leaving the hospital and living in lodgings rather than returning home with parents. He also noted, however, that a patient staying with his mother had a reduced risk of relapse if the mother worked outside of the home.[22]

The reason for these relapses, Brown argues, is due to criticism, hostility, and "emotional over-involvement" which "manifests itself by over-emotionality, excessive self-sacrifice, over-identification, and extreme overprotective behavior with the patient."[23] In some circumstances, a parent remembers their child "before" a particular onset and can sometimes find themselves desperately longing for their child to return to the person they once were. Sometimes it is easier to foster a spirit of non-anxious compassion for nonfamily members.

Our deepest understandings of love tend to emerge from relationships of mutual recognition. Ironically enough, it is *because* of these bonds of love that we often have difficulty finding mutual recognition within trauma. When I enter into the trauma of the other, I am doing so with the knowledge that I am somehow intertwined within this narrative—even if it's merely as a bystander to one that I love. Judith Butler explains: "a narrative that responds to allegation must, from the outset, accept the possibility that the self has causal agency, even if, in a given instance, the self may not have been the cause of the suffering in question."[24] It is possible that for some, this mutual recognition is too painful to bear—the individual is unable to hear the pain of another without the immediate introspection that turns toward an inner world of shame and fear. Drawing from Nietzsche, Butler explains:

> He remarks that we become conscious of ourselves only after certain injuries have been inflicted. Someone suffers as a consequence, and the suffering person or, rather, someone acting as his or her advocate in a system of justice seeks to find the cause of that suffering and asks whether we might be that cause. . . . In asking whether we caused such suffering, we are being asked by an established authority not only to avow a causal link between our own actions and the suffering that follows but also to take responsibility for these actions and their effects. In this context, we find ourselves in the position of having to give an account of ourselves . . . we become reflective upon ourselves, accordingly, through fear and terror.[25]

When hearing a story of trauma, it can be difficult to move outside of fear and blame and serve as a non-anxious presence. Yes, it is possible the person in pain will implicitly or explicitly incriminate me for her pain, but it is also possible she is simply looking for a witness to her trauma.[26] The mothers who were not engaged in recognition of their daughters were still contributing to the narrative in their silence. Butler explains:

> The refusal to narrate remains a relation to narrative and to the scene of address. As a narrative withheld, it either refuses the relation that the inquirer

presupposes or changes that relation so that the one queried refuses the one who queries.[27]

RECOGNITION IN DEPTH

Perhaps first and foremost, recognition is presence. Recognition involves a non-anxious presence that can sit with trauma without attempting to fix, master, disprove, or use the events of others. It listens to the past and it attends to the future, but it resides in the present with another human being beside me. Recognition is the mutual gaze of equals that says, "I see you. You see me." And subsequently, "And I see me because you see me." Recognition is not a spectator of pain, but a witness to it. And the witness I bear has an indelible effect upon my personhood. We create space for articulation when our words and actions communicate: "I see you."[28]

There is an old, Eastern story that's been told in various ways and is applicable here. It goes something like this:

> There was an old man who worked the land as a farmer. One day, a horse that he owned ran away. "Oh no," cried his neighbors, "What horrible luck," they said.
> "Maybe it is, maybe it isn't," the farmer replied.
> The next day the stallion returned with three other wild horses.
> "Oh my!" came the reply of the neighbors, "What wonderful luck!"
> "Maybe it is, maybe it isn't," the farmer replied.
> The day next the farmer's son was riding one of the wild horses and was thrown off and broke his leg.
> "Oh no," cried his neighbors, "What horrible luck," they said.
> "Maybe it is, maybe it isn't," the farmer replied.
> The next day war broke out across the land and all of the young men were rounded off and sent off to fight. The farmer's son was passed over due to his injured leg.
> "Oh my!" came the reply of the neighbors, "What wonderful luck!"
> "Maybe it is, maybe it isn't," the farmer replied.[29]

The farmer in this story isn't hiding from pain or sugarcoating it; rather, he is holding his experiences loosely with open palms, willing to see what comes without pronouncing it good or bad. It simply is.

My previous work on testimony speaks to the need of speaking with a language of humility where statements are couched in words like "maybe" or "I wonder if." The story above takes this understanding further and invites its listeners to a continual state of presence where one is aware of what is going on, but is not quick to assign meaning.

WHAT RECOGNITION IS *NOT*

Sometimes it is easier to understand what something *is* by understanding what something is *not*. So, while the concept of recognition will be further explored in later chapters, it is worth briefly noting the following:

1. *Recognition does not require agreement.* It is possible to recognize someone without agreeing with their current position. I might have deep empathy for my child who throws a fit when he sees his neighbor's new bicycle and shoves his friend. I see his longing and jealousy. I recognize the embarrassment he might feel over his own bike and its dents and dings. I recognize the subsequent shame that often follows an outburst of this sort. I can recognize my son's feelings and offer compassion without agreeing with or condoning his actions.
2. *Recognition does not preclude consequences.* Just because I recognize the deep longing and pain my child has expressed toward the neighbor's new bicycle, this recognition does not bind me from creating boundaries or consequences for these actions.
3. *Recognition does not require a solution.* I was traveling with a small group of students to a conference when the subject of racism emerged. A distant colleague asked a student what kinds of conversations on racism were occurring on our college campus and with great angst this student replied that while there were numerous conversations about race, he didn't know what to do with them. "I kept asking who I could apologize to, but . . . ." His voice trailed off as he shrugged. This well-intended student conflated recognition with solutions. He had caught a dimension of a problem and wanted to fix it. And when he became aware of just how large and systemic the problem was—one he had no hope of fixing by himself—he walked away from the subject at hand. But recognition does not require fixing. In fact, recognition often involves what may look like a *passivity* that primarily receives. Sometimes recognition looks less like a solution and more like a lament. While the traumatic event calling for recognition may involve very intense emotions, recognition often involves a kind of non-anxious presence that says, "This is unbearable and I am here next to you." Recognition in this case is the attempt to linger over what agitates you, knowing that the Holy Spirit is hovering above the chaos.[30] When I, as a white woman, linger on the periphery of

the pain that my sisters and brothers of color experience I believe I am drawing near to the heart of God.
4. *Recognition does not require details or knowledge before it can be given.* Social media was buzzing with laments and confusion when Trayvon Martin was shot and killed in February 2012. There were questions and cries and anger over the loss of life of this teenager. It seemed like there were three primary responses to the death of Trayvon Martin (all highly simplified here): (1) those who were angered and heartbroken over this death, (2) those who thought the actions of George Zimmerman were justified, and (3) those who refrained from engaging in dialogue until more facts were known. Within this third group is a subset that suggests that the rest of us should avoid speaking as well until we know more.

This third subset bothers me. Those who take this stance may assume they are being impartial, when in fact their noncommittal words often serve as a kind of grandstanding by saying nothing. They might think they are carving out space and time for properly vetted "facts" to emerge, but in fact, they are often engaging in nonrecognition. This is a mindset that falsely believes one needs information in order to recognize another.[31] Embedded within this stance is a false sense of neutrality. Desmond Tutu captures this sentiment beautifully: "If you are neutral in situations of injustice, you have chosen the side of the oppressor. If an elephant has its foot on the tail of a mouse and you say that you are neutral, the mouse will not appreciate your neutrality."[32] Sometimes a person assumes this position because they are afraid of being wrong, the rationale being, "What if I speak up and then find out later that I was mistaken? Perhaps I'd better just be quiet until we know more." It is often people in power who assume this position. As a white, educated woman one could argue that I have the "luxury" of refraining from recognizing the death of Trayvon Martin. This luxury is certainly not extended to the African American teenager who is walking down the street in a hoodie. I can withhold judgment. I can remain silent. I am not in immediate danger by simply sticking my head in the sand. However, this is not a viable option for people of color in the United States. Charles Blow of the New York Times shares some haunting sentiments:

> As a parent, particularly a parent of black teenage boys, I am left with the question, "Now, what do I tell my boys?"
>
> We used to say not to run in public because that might be seen as suspicious, like they'd stolen something. But according to Zimmerman, Martin drew his suspicion at least in part because he was walking too slowly.
>
> So what do I tell my boys now? At what precise pace should a black man walk to avoid suspicion?[33]

I can attempt to ignore the story. Charles M. Blow cannot. The value of black lives is not contingent on details, evidence, or drug tests. Black lives matter. Rebuttals or assertions that "All Lives Matter," while true, is functionally an act of nonrecognition. You are telling me something but I refuse to listen. Recognition is not a zero-sum game. The recognition of one person does not take away from the recognition of another.

Recognition does not require details or certain knowledge before it can be given. In chapter 4 we read the story of Rachel who experiences deep and meaningful recognition from her community following her sexual assault. While the community knew of the assault, even basic details were not widely known, nor were they needed in order to offer recognition.

5. *Recognition is not a means to an end.* A while back I was speaking at an event out of state when I ran into an old friend. He was someone I had looked up to, and he was currently serving as a pastor—I'll call him Pastor X. We had not seen each other in some time, and he inquired about the scandal within my extended family from the previous summer.[34] 'I shared tentatively, hesitantly, not sure how much I wanted to disclose. He asked deep and insightful questions, and I found myself responding with gratitude. The type of questions he asked left me feeling known and understood. With great empathy, he asked questions about a particular individual who had hurt me. How was it possible to forgive him after what he did? Did I have any sense of what a healing journey might look like? I was grateful for his questions up until his closing comment. I was minutes away from walking on stage to speak, when Pastor X concluded by saying, "Thanks so much for sharing. I'm preaching a sermon on betrayal this weekend and I can totally use this. I think God meant for us to connect."

This man had misrecognized my trauma as a sermon illustration. I wish I'd had a firm, clear response to him indicating my insistence on keeping my story private, but instead I froze. I was conscious of my impending lecture and was afraid to do anything that might release the tears I could feel forming. I kept quiet and watched him walk away with my story.

The irony of the situation was lost on him.

Consider now how my encounter with this friend becomes wrapped up in a single experience. Originally it looked as follows:

Event: the subject of our conversation was the traumatic events that had occurred in my life.

Articulation: As Pastor X asked more and more questions I began to share with him not only what had happened, but how I was processing those events.

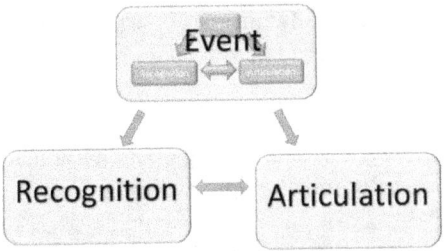

Figure 2.1 Articulacy Loop as "Event."

Recognition: Pastor X misrecognized my trauma as a story he could use for his own purposes.

This entire encounter with Pastor X then becomes a single experience (see figure 2.1). And so after Pastor X leaves and my lecture is over, I turn to my friend Elaine, who is traveling with me, and tell her somewhat hesitantly what has just taken place with Pastor X. My entire encounter with Pastor X is now the event that I articulate to my friend. She hears me speak of this event and responds with horrified gasps and statements of support. The way in which Elaine recognizes my encounter with Pastor X changes the way that I articulate this experience. My initial reporting to my friend was done with hesitation and shame—that a mere conversation that had taken place an hour ago still had an emotional grip on me. Elaine's recognition, however, changed the way in which I now articulate this experience. I am affirmed in my reaction, my pain suddenly seems more justified, and I feel a little less embarrassed by my tears.

Imagine, however, that I shared this experience with Elaine and was met with blank stares, or she responded with a seemingly trivial comparison. Her response may impact what I share with others in the future, as well as how I interpret the situation myself.

Along with that self-justification, however, came the painful realization that I undoubtedly was guilty of inflicting this kind of pain on others. Elaine's recognition of my pain triggered the realization that surely there have been times in my life when I had used other people's stories in my own sermons or lectures in order to make a point. It was an embodiment of the earlier quote from Butler channeling Nietzsche, "that we become conscious of ourselves only after certain injuries have been inflicted. Someone suffers as a consequence, and the suffering person or, rather, someone acting as his or her advocate in a system of justice seeks to find the cause of that suffering and asks whether we might be that cause."[35] I remember a friend telling me soon after, "Oh, I never tell Pastor X anything about my problems. I'd be too afraid it would show up in a sermon with some pseudonym that would leave everyone knowing that it was me he was actually talking about."³⁶ In other words, this man was afraid of his story being exploited or used.

6. *Recognition is not pity.* When hearing about a traumatic event, one might have a tendency to unintentionally patronize another by showing pity. The person in this position tends to engage as a spectator, observing the calamity that has come upon this other person. Pity says: "You are there. I am here. I am not in the pain with you, and because of that I will comfort you from a distance as I remain planted in my own emotional security." Pity tends to keep us either in the past or projects us into the future. In the first instance, I am focused on the events of the past which sound so horrific to me. In the second, my pity transitions to fear thinking, "I hope that never happens to me." There is a condescension that is wrapped up in pity that is missing in recognition. Aboriginal Activist Lila Watson captures this sentiment beautifully: "If you have come here to help me, you are wasting your time. But if you have come because your liberation is bound up with mine, then let us work together."³⁷

What Is Recognition?

If recognition withheld is oppression, a fitting conclusion might be that recognition granted is freedom. Speaking of the master/slave dialectic, Hegelian philosopher Robert R. Williams explains: "What each seeks is not the recognition of the mere fact of his existence but the recognition of his freedom."³⁸ Love and recognition are interrelated, and I am known via my connection with another. Williams quotes Hegel saying, "Love is the consciousness of my unity with another so that I am not isolated by myself, but gain my self-consciousness only in the renunciation of my independence, and by knowing myself in relation and union with another."³⁹

Conclusion: A Story of Recognition

In my first semester of seminary I had significant stomach problems. There were doctor visits, medications prescribed, and multiple visits to the hospital. It was around that time when I read a particular book on prayer. The author was making the claim that since God is our father, surely he wants good things for us and that we should simply ask for what we want with great tenacity. Keep asking, the author reasoned, he's your father. And so I did. I started praying when I felt the first twinge of a stomach attack. I prayed as I lay down to try to sleep it off. I prayed as I emptied my stomach over and over. I prayed on the way to the emergency room. I prayed for eight hours straight.

When I left the hospital the next morning I was not praying. I stopped somewhere between the saline IV and the morphine drip. I left feeling foolish. I remember having the mental image of prayers wafting up like bubbles toward heaven, only to hit the ceiling and pop. My prayers seemed as ridiculous as rubbing a bottle, hoping a genie would emerge.

A day later I was walking in a quiet alley through the seminary campus. It was October and the leaves had changed. The air was crisp. I walked through the alley with a keen awareness of the spiritual emptiness I felt.

As I walked, I saw a single leaf slowly float to the ground. It was one of those massive, colorful leafs—so big it was almost its own parachute. The wind was taking it back and forth, back and forth as it floated toward the ground. The leaf caught my eye, and as I watched it falling slowly, I sensed three words: "I see you." That was it. No promise of healing, no reassurance of my character or religious sensibilities. Just, "I see you." And for whatever reason, that short and simple phrase removed my shame and left me with the impression that while my prayers were not answered, God had seen me. This alleyway was my spring in the desert, and I could now echo the words of Hagar: "You are the God who sees me."[40] And I was surprised to realize that for me that was enough for now.

NOTES

1. When we encounter a traumatic event, *if* we are able to find space to articulate that trauma and *if* our trauma is appropriately recognized, we are able to better integrate our pain into the narratives of our lives. The inability to integrate traumatic experiences into our lives is what makes trauma particularly disorienting. Theologian Shelly Rambo puts it this way: "Suffering is what, in time, can be integrated into one's understanding of the world. Trauma is what is not integrated in time; it is the difference between a closed and an open wound." Rambo, *Spirit and Trauma*, 7.

2. This Sunday night group was under the auspices of College Wesleyan Church in Marion, Indiana. I am particularly thankful to Rev. Judy Crossman, PhD, for her willingness to provide oversight.

3. I'm grateful for these ten women who graciously allowed me to share parts of their stories. Additionally, I'm grateful for the seven who agreed to take part in extensive interviews following our first year together.

4. It is worth noting that there are people who may find a doctor's office a difficult place in which to articulate her needs. For whatever reason, the individual is intimidated and finds herself freezing and forgetting to ask the pressing questions that brought her there in the first place.

5. "Philosophy is perfectly right in saying that life must be understood backward. But then one forgets the other clause—that it must be lived forward. The more one thinks through this clause, the more one concludes that life in temporality never becomes properly understandable, simply because never at any time does one get perfect repose to take a stance—backward." Howard V. Hong and Edna H. Hong, *The Essential Kierkegaard* (Princeton: Princeton University Press, 2000), 12.

6. In addition to the fear of speaking, one might also be of the mindset that talking is superfluous. "What good is talking about it? It's not like anyone can fix it at this point. It still happened." While I will be arguing for the significance of articulation, I would be remiss to not include a conversation on the role of *redistribution* within recognition. Nancy Fraser and Axel Honneth raise important critiques within what they see as limitations of recognition. While I believe a more robust definition of recognition helps identify some of the problems they raise, their critiques nevertheless deserve attention. Nancy Fraser and Axel Honneth, *Redistribution and Recognition: A Political-Philosophical Exchange* (London: Verso, 2003).

7. We did not call them "rites of recognition" at the time. They were simply "things to do."

8. With very little exception, these rites of recognition have revolved around various forms of beauty and creativity. Justice can often seem elusive in cases of trauma. If a woman is raped and her attacker is caught and imprisoned, has the survivor truly experienced justice? What does justice even look like when certain acts cannot be undone? It makes sense that in cases like these, the desire for beauty may rise to the surface—this kind of longing for something that transcends the pain.

9. The question of whether or not one needs another individual in order to recognize one's self is a well-contested question in academia. Feminist critiques, accusations of essentialism, and the dangers of subjectivism give readers pause to continually keep the question, "What is recognition?" in the foreground. See Lois McNay, *Against Recognition* (Cambridge: Polity, 2008). Arto Laitinen, "Interpersonal Recognition: A Response to Value or Precondition of Personhood," *Inquiry*, 45 (2002): 463–78. Markell Patchen. *Bound by Recognition* (New Jersey: Princeton University Press, 2003).

10. Woman 3. Interview by Amanda Hontz Drury. Written transcript. Marion, Indiana, February 16, 2014.

11. "[T]he road to interiority passes through the other." Robert R. Williams, *Recognition: Fichte and Hegel on the Other* (Albany, NY: State University of New York Press, 1992), 151.

12. A nod to Phyllis Tribles's *Texts of Terror: Literary Feminist Readings of Biblical Narratives*. (Minneapolis: Fortress Press), 1984.

13. 2 Samuel 13:14.

14. There are numerous studies connecting the rise of empathy to hearing another person's story. While a great deal of this literature focuses on the fictional stories that garner empathy, more recent scholarship has explored how empathy arises when we hear nonfiction accounts from people around us. Jennings Bryant and Dolf Zillmann in "Empathy: Affect from Bearing Witness to the Emotions of Others" in *Responding to the Screen, Reception and Reaction Processes* (Hillsdale, NJ: L. Erlbaum Associates, 1991), 135–68.

15. Woman 2.
16. Woman 5.
17. Martin L. Anderson describes the empathetic connections that emerge between speaker and listener. He writes that this empathy is "a largely involuntary, vicarious response to affective cues from another person or from his situation." Martin L. Anderson, "A Three Component Model of Empathy" (Paper presented at the Biennial Meeting of the Society for Research in Child Development, New Orleans, Louisiana, March 17–20, 1977). This paper is available on microfiche at http://files.eric.ed.gov/fulltext/ED139514.pdf, accessed November 21, 2016.
18. Suzanne Keen speaks of a "primitive emotional contagion" which prompts those receiving our narratives to mirror the expressions of the speaker. Suzanne Keen, "A Theory of Narrative Empathy," *Narrative* 14, no 3 (October 2006): 209.
19. Adrienne Rich, *On Lies, Secrets, and Silence: Selected Prose 1966–1978* (New York: Norton, 1979), 192.
20. Anekal C. Amaresha and Ganesan Venkatasubramanian, "Expressed Emotion in Schizophrenia: An Overview," Indiana Journal of Psychological Medicine 34, no. 1 (January–March 2012): 12–20, accessed July 23, 2018, https://www.ncbi.nlm.nih.gov/pmc/articles/PMC3361836/.
21. Amaresha and Ganesan, "Expressed Emotion," 12–20.
22. Amaresha and Ganesan, "Expressed Emotion," 12–20.
23. "Parents of a child, who develops schizophrenia, always feel guilty for the child's illness. This chronic guilt leads them to initiate reparative efforts to make things better for the child, and in its extreme form can signify the overprotectiveness for the sick person. Unfortunately, this has the effect of discouraging the person's skills and self-reliance, so that in the long run, overprotectiveness hampers the person's recovery. It also leads to dependence of the patient on their caregiver. The patient then becomes worried about the outlook of having to cope without the continuous support of their caregiver and becomes dependent. This EOI is most commonly shown by parents, especially mothers, and occasionally by fathers, but rarely by other relatives." Amaresha and Ganesan, "Expressed Emotion," 12–20.
24. Judith Butler, *Giving an Account*, 12.
25. Butler, *Giving an Account*, 10–11.
26. See Andrew Root on place-sharing in *Revisiting Relational Youth Ministry: From a Strategy of Influence to a Theology of Incarnation* (Downers Grove: InterVaristy Press, 2007).
27. Butler softens and expands Nietzsche's understanding of the role of fear in mutual recognition by suggesting that there are "valences besides fear. There may well be a desire to know and understand that is not fueled by the desire to punish, and a desire to explain and narrate that is not prompted by the terror of punishment." Butler, *Giving an Account*, 12.
28. "When those who have the power to name and to socially construct reality choose not to see you or hear you, whether you are dark-skinned, old, disabled, female, or speak with a different accent or dialect than theirs, when someone with the authority of a teacher, say, describes the world and you are not in it, there is a moment of psychic disequilibrium, as if you looked into a mirror and saw nothing." Adrienne Rich, "Invisibility in Academe" *Blood, Bread and Poetry* (New York: Norton, 1986), 199.

29. The above is my version of an old Taoist story that appears in multiple versions in multiple sources.

30. Spiritual director and author Sharon Garlough Brown has been a key voice for me regarding maintaining a non-anxious presence. She instructs her readers to "learn to linger with what provokes you. You may just find the Spirit of God moving there." *Sensible Shoes: A Story About the Spiritual Journey* (Downers Grove, IL: InterVarsity Press, 2013), 80.

31. This is not to suggest that we never seek more information—we often have very good and just reasons for pursuing truth. The point here, however, is that recognition does not hinge on information.

32. Desmond Tutu as quoted by Robert McAfee Brown, *Unexpected News: Reading the Bible with Third World Eyes* (Philadelphia: Westminster Press, 1984), 19.

33. Charles M. Blow "The Whole System Failed Trayvon Martin," The New York Times, July 15, 2013. Accessed October 13, 2016. http://www.nytimes.com/2013/07/16/opinion/the-whole-system-failed.html?_r=0.

34. See introduction.

35. Butler, *Giving an Account of Oneself*, 10, 11.

36. Just to be clear, this friend gave me permission to share this story in this chapter.

37. While this comment has been attributed to one of Watson's speeches, she claims she is not comfortable taking the credit for a statement she says came out of a collective process within Aboriginal activist groups.

38. Williams, *Hegel's Ethics of Recognition*, 60.

39. Williams, *Hegel's Ethics of Recognition*, 212.

40. Genesis 16:13.

Theological Interlude 2
Feeding the Enemy

FEEDING THE ENEMY

Not long ago I was reading through a particular passage of Scripture with a woman who had experienced significant trauma. 2 Kings tells a mind-boggling story of the prophet Elisha waking up one morning and realizing he is surrounded by enemies. His servant is terrified, but Elisha tells him not to be afraid and reveals that there are horses and chariots of fire from God surrounding the enemy. The Lord blinds the enemy, and Elisha emerges as an Obi-Wan Kenobi type figure telling them, "These are not the droids you're looking for," and instead leads the blinded enemy directly into Samaria where the king of Israel resides. The eyes of the enemies are opened and they are terrified to find themselves at the mercy of the king. Rather than killing his enemy, however, the king of Israel prepares a feast for his enemies. He wines and dines them and sends them on their way.[1]

The woman almost interrupted the ending of the story with her own pressing question: "But Mandy, how can I feed my enemy? What in the world would it look like for me to feed this man?"

I recoiled at the thought of this dear woman returning to this dangerous man, and I felt a flash of anger toward those in the church who would have pushed this woman back to this man as if the commandment given was not "Love your neighbor as yourself," but "Love your neighbor *instead of* yourself."

I suggested that perhaps she wasn't yet at the end of the story. Perhaps she was just at the beginning. Maybe her prayer for the present was not "Help me to feed my enemies," but "God, please blind the eyes of my enemy and let me witness your presence."

Those of us who are preachers have a tendency to bring people right up to the end of the story. We come to the end and say, "Now go and do likewise." We leave the story quite tidy. But we would be wise to consider Rambo's language of the middle—to create space for the poison in the wound to seep out.

What does it mean to minister in the middle of texts of trauma? It means we acknowledge the deep pain and anguish of saints of the past. We provide space for people today to identify with that trauma. We draw attention to the middle, sitting with the tension perhaps longer than our typical comfort levels would allow. We reimagine endings with hope that perhaps life might still come out of this chaos. Our job is to draw out these texts of trauma and infuse hope while giving permission to the survivor to wait in the middle. This means we move slower than many of us would like. We are slower to find resolution. As the old adage says, "The slower you go, the sooner you get there."

Consider the laments of the Psalms. Psalm 77 in particular speaks of a God who slams the door on compassion, who has forgotten to be kind, and whose promises have turned to curses. When we look for texts of trauma throughout the entirety of Scripture, we are left with this conclusion: there is a place for me here in my pain. I can claim Jesus as my Lord and Savior and still feel as if I have the sentence of death in my heart. There is room for me here. I can attest to the risen Lord and still acknowledge the depth of my own pain and suffering.

NOTE

1. 2 Kings 6:8–23.

Chapter 3

Event

Jacob's Story

It is more than a little unsettling to come to the conclusion that watching your child's skull get fractured by a horse is the *easy* part of your story. Nevertheless, this is where Sarah found herself during the summer of 2011.[1] On July 4th, Sarah and her family were visiting friends who raised 4-H horses. Sarah knew them to be gentle horses and followed her children into the barn to greet them.

At some point during their visit, the horses became spooked and began to scatter. Sarah explains what took place next:

> I didn't know where Jacob was right at the moment when they started to scatter, but I turned around and saw him on the ground and a horse running over top of him. And the horse sort of paused with Jacob under his feet. I think the horse was trying to figure out what to do . . . I saw [Jacob] get kicked in the back of the head. He knocked Jacob back and forth a few times with his hoof under his feet and then took off running. I remember that moment very clearly.[2]

Sarah explains: "I saw everything in slow motion and I saw Jacob get flipped forward and flipped backward, and I just was thinking, 'This is bad. This is really bad.' I know it just happened in a second, but it seemed like a minute long."

Sarah's husband, David, reached Jacob first, scooped him up, and took him out of the corral. It was at this point, Sarah explains, that she came out of the slow-motion feeling and returned to real time. Sarah drew upon her fifteen years as a trauma nurse in the ER and did a quick assessment. Everything looked normal—Jacob was conscious, and there was no bruising or blood of any sort. Nevertheless, owing to the serious nature of the injury, Sarah and David took Jacob to the emergency room.

On the way to the ER, he started feeling really sick to his stomach and was stating that things sounded really loud to him. He kept covering his ears and so I was a little concerned that he had a head injury because of the nausea.... We got him to the ER and they took him right back and did a CT scan... the CT scan of Jacob's brain looked great but he had a skull fracture. And because of the skull fracture, and because he continued to have a lot of nausea and vomiting, he needed to be admitted. So he was taken by Lutheran ambulance transfer service to the pediatric ward at the Lutheran hospital. He was in the hospital for three days.

For the most part, Jacob's stay in the ICU was uneventful. Friends and family visited, meals and toys were brought, and Jacob was soon released with a clean bill of health and instructions to take it easy for the rest of the summer.

We thought everything was great and were so thankful that Jacob was spared physically. I knew from being a nurse in the ICU how bad it could have been.... We were told he had a concussion [and] to keep the stimuli really low. His little wings were completely clipped that summer, he wasn't allowed to ride his bike. David had just built a treehouse in the backyard that he wasn't allowed to go up into because they didn't want him to fall from any distance whatsoever. We started introducing things back slowly.

It was a full two weeks later when problems started to emerge. Both Sarah and her husband were working weekend shifts, and Sarah's mother offered to take the kids to church on Sunday morning. What happened next is worth reading at length:

After two weeks, I felt like it'd be good for him to get back into a routine. And at that point he was bragging to the others. At one point he said, "I got kicked by a horse, and not even superheroes get kicked by horses." So he was feeling pretty tough. I thought that things were going really well. I told my mom to go ahead and take him to church and maybe just keep an extra eye on him and see how it goes.

That evening my mom called me on my way home and said, "We had a small incident today." She said that during church, something had set off the fire alarms. [There was a] siren noise and flashing lights, and she said that Jacob absolutely panicked. She said that he started crying hysterically and screaming and running around. And Jacob of all three of my kids is by far the most laid back. It takes a lot to get him excited about anything. I thought that was strange but figured he was just a little more sensitive because of everything he'd gone through. She said it took her a while to get him calmed down. He was really upset.

I asked him that night what happened, and he just said that the fire alarms went off at church and that it was really scary. I said that I was really sorry about that, and he just went off and played so I thought everything was ok.

A few days after that I just noticed some subtle changes with him. . . . He wanted [all the lights] to be on and for me to go with him to the end of the hallway to his bedroom every time he needed something. And that was definitely a change for him. He also asked me to go with him to the bathroom. And so, the changes started out really slow and subtle. . . . At first it was an annoyance, like, "Come on Jacob; you don't need me to go with you to the bathroom." Sometimes he'd keep the door open and sometimes he just wouldn't go unless I went with him. And then it started to worsen a little bit. . . . Three or four weeks after the accident, it started to get worse. . . . The first week after the fire alarm incident it was him not wanting to go anywhere without me and wanting all the lights on. And the next week it progressed and he started seeing smoke . . . I'd put him to bed . . . and he would call me, screaming. Just panicking and screaming. I'd run to his room and I'd say, "What's the matter Jacob? What's going on?" And he'd say, "The room is on fire! The room is on fire!" I'd ask him what he meant and that there was no fire, and he'd say that he saw smoke and he knew there was smoke.

One time he said that there was smoke behind the bedroom door and so I flipped on the lights and looked and said, "Look, Buddy, there's no smoke." And he'd look and claim that there was smoke. . . . This would continue night after night. He would say he saw smoke everywhere. And I'm not sure how long it was after that, but he started having really terrible thoughts. He would be afraid. . . . A month after the original accident . . . he was afraid to go out to the garage to get something that I asked him to go get . . . I said, "What's going on, Buddy? Why don't you want to go out there?" He said, "What if there is a man out there who is going to shoot me?" And I just felt my heart sink because I thought, "Where is this coming from? Where is he getting this from?" All the sudden this was getting really weird really fast. I didn't know what was going on.

Jacob was extremely fixated at the time with making sure that all of the smoke detectors in the house had been checked. Everywhere we went in public, he'd point out the smoke detectors and sprinkler systems. He'd say, "This place has a nice sprinkler system," which is really strange coming from a six-year-old. . . . Some [stores] he wouldn't go into if I didn't reassure him that they had a smoke detector. I told him that every store has to have them according to the law. He said, "What if they didn't change the batteries?"

It got really dark. One time he said, "I had a dream last night that we pulled out of the driveway, and there was a man waiting for us and shot us all and we looked down and there were holes in our bodies and blood coming out." There were times that I would just cry because I had tried very hard to block my kids from violence on TV which is hard to do these days . . . I couldn't figure out where he was coming up with these dark visions that he was having . . .

One night he called me into his room screaming. I went in there and he said he couldn't sleep and [when] I asked him why . . . he said "the pile of blankets; there's a little kid under the blankets and he's waiting for me to fall asleep and then he'll shoot me." And I said, "Jacob, that's not the truth," and we'd look. I told him about how we could pray, and Jesus would keep us safe, and it didn't really seem to matter what I said; he was extremely distraught all the time that someone was going to shoot him, or the house was going to burn down.

Sarah began contemplating whether or not her son had early onset schizophrenia. She entered a dark place herself feeling completely powerless to help her son.

I felt like I should know what to do. I thought, here I am a medical professional, and I should know what to do. But I have no idea what to do. I almost wish that his skull had been fractured, and they would have had to have surgery . . . and they could have just fixed it, and we would be done and over. Because in that world at least I'd be comfortable with it. I was comfortable knowing that I felt like I knew what the outcome would be. I felt like I was thrown into a world that I knew nothing about. I felt very helpless. I cried a lot. I just thought, "Oh my gosh, my child is going crazy. I'm going to have a kid who's crazy for the rest of our lives now." I was completely devastated. I just felt like we were spiraling out of control.

And then came Jacob's six-week follow-up appointment with the neurologist. The appointment, Sarah explains, "was a five minute 'Let me feel your head . . . have you had any vomiting? His pupils look good.'" The doctor then asked if she had any concerns. Sarah shared some of her concerns about the changes in Jacob and was directed across the hall to the psychiatrist to discuss the possibility of post-traumatic stress disorder (PTSD). All of a sudden, Sarah said, things began to "click." And a small light appeared in their dark tunnel.

THE TRAUMATIC EVENT

The story of Jacob and the horse is an almost textbook example of PTSD. Words like "stress" and "trauma" are often used in our everyday conversations, though certainly not in their clinical senses—a deadline stresses us out. A confusing relationship status brings out our stress. The looming graduation date is just plain stressful. The word "trauma" pops up as well—oftentimes in playful and facetious ways. We might speak of the traumatic as a way of exaggerating a situation for humor's sake. The squirt of ketchup on the shirt?

Traumatic. That midterm report? Traumatic. The prospects of Valentine's Day alone? Trauma. Trauma. Trauma.

We indiscriminately throw these words around—seldom in relationship with one another. Put the two words together, however, "traumatic stress" and all of a sudden, we have a particular condition that, while not often spoken of, is quite common.

It is worth repeating our working definition of a traumatic experience as *"one in which a person or persons perceives themselves or others as threatened by an external force that seeks to annihilate them and against which they are unable to resist and which overwhelms their capacity to cope."*[3] Again, it is important to stress that this occurs if the person feels as if an external force is threatening them. It does not matter if, in fact, they are safe; if they *perceive* this threat as dangerous it is considered traumatic.[4]

Consider the trauma that can occur in everyday car accidents. Imagine a person driving along the road who hits a patch of ice and finds herself careering through traffic lanes directly into oncoming traffic. There is an outside force that is threatening her that she is completely unable to control and has overwhelmed her capacity to cope. Her life flashes before her eyes. Traumatic stress. Let's assume the car manages to come to a stop and she is safe. The hope is that once her heart resumes its normal pace, she is able to recognize that the threat has past. She is safe and the traumatic stress is over. That is the best-case scenario.

It is possible, however, that this traumatic stress will develop into *post-traumatic stress*, and the woman finds her heart pounding every time she sits behind the wheel. The immediate threat of the car accident is over, but the post-traumatic stress remains and driving a vehicle is now a major obstacle to work through. She carries on with normal life and seems to function well—except for when she needs to drive somewhere. She sits in the car and finds herself reliving her brush with death—oftentimes with physical manifestations of this stress.

Of course, sometimes post-traumatic stress becomes even more sinister and she develops PTSD. Her fear of driving has bled into other areas of her life, and she finds herself barely able to cope despite the fact that she is sitting behind a desk, not behind the wheel.

In a similar vein, consider again six-year-old Jacob who has been trampled by a horse and is now terrified of fire.

JACOB GOES TO COUNSELING

Sarah and Jacob met with the hospital psychiatrist and were ultimately referred to a trauma counselor by the name of Felicia Snell a few towns over.[5] Sarah oscillated between fear that the counselor couldn't help Jacob and self-doubt as she wondered whether or not she was simply blowing things out of proportion.

"It's like when you take your kids to the doctor and all of the sudden they're totally normal. I was afraid that we would get there to see her, and he wouldn't open up, and he'd be totally normal, and then she couldn't help us."

They arrived at the counselor's office and sat in the waiting room while Felicia finished up with a client. When the counselor emerged from her office and introduced herself, the very first words out of Jacob's mouth were, "I see you don't have any smoke detectors in your office." Sarah immediately thought, "Oh my gosh, this whole time we've been sitting here, and he's been looking around for smoke detectors." The counselor showed Jacob where the smoke detectors were and then invited him and Sarah into her office.

Felicia asked Jacob to describe what he remembered being under the horse. Jacob immediately described the clouds of dust that surrounded him during the incident. Somehow, for Jacob, the dust of the horse and the potential smoke from the fire alarm triggered something within him. Felicia explained to Sarah that oftentimes with children, it's a secondary event that triggers the PTSD. In this case, the traumatic event was getting trampled by the horse, with the secondary event being the piercing fire alarm at church.

Jacob began bi-weekly appointments where Felicia employed EMDR, a method of therapy often used in PTSD that helps the brain process traumatic memories.[6] Sarah describes it this way: "[The counselor] told me . . . your brain is like a filing cabinet and the trauma is like this folder that the brain doesn't know what to do with. It doesn't know where to put it. EMDR would help the brain try to categorize it and where to put it in the brain." The counselor explained that this kind of therapy tended to be very exhausting for kids, and sure enough, ten minutes into the drive home, Jacob fell asleep and slept the entire ninety-minute journey home.

TRAUMA AND THE BRAIN

Traumatic events—again, those unstoppable events that threaten to annihilate and overwhelm our abilities to cope—are stored differently in our brains than non-traumatic events.[7] Our brains have a difficult time categorizing and storing traumatic memories. Put simply, the right and left sides of the brain are not able to effectively communicate back and forth in order to properly store the traumatic memory, and in this way trauma differs from suffering. It is almost like traumatic events serve as tiny shocks to our brain's storage systems. The EMDR sessions that Jacob began helped integrate the traumatic experience into the fabric of his brain. The goal was not to make him forget the event, but rather to be able to remember the event without the charged response.

Jacob's CT scan showed a fractured skull and an otherwise healthy brain. What it could not show, however, were the subsequent changes taking place in his locus coeruleus (or LC), that part of the brainstem responsible for physiological responses to stress. PTSD prompts a continuous arousal in the autonomic nervous system. Your autonomic nervous system is what regulates the functions of your internal organs as well as certain muscles within your body. It is your autonomic nervous system that assesses a situation and instructs your body how to respond accordingly. For example, in an emergency situation, your autonomic nervous system can instruct your body toward fight, flight, or freeze. In non-emergency situations, it can tell your body to rest and relax.

In PTSD, however, one's autonomic nervous system is in a *constant* state of arousal. So even though one might be in a perfectly safe environment without any threat, the body cannot relax because the brain is still sending signals of pending danger.

I toured Israel when I was fifteen. Somewhere along the way I turned an ankle and while it didn't seem to be serious, by the time I arrived back home I was in a lot of pain. In addition to swelling, my foot felt like it was burning yet was still cool to the touch. I was barely able to walk, but all x-rays and scans of my foot looked completely normal. It took a few months for me to get my diagnosis: Reflex Sympathetic Dystrophy (RSD). The way I understand my experience with RSD in non-medical terms is this: after an initial, minor injury to my foot, the nerves in my brain continued to send the signal that my foot was injured. Even after the muscles and ligaments had healed, my brain kept reacting as if my foot was injured. There was nothing wrong with my foot, but my brain thought otherwise. Once the diagnosis was made, the goal became to disrupt the pain cycle—to numb the firing nerves just long enough for my brain to figure out the hypervigilance was unnecessary. After a single spinal block, I watched a thermometer slowly move up multiple degrees, bringing my foot back to room temperature. Furthermore, the pain subsided—even after the nerve block had worn off.

A similar kind of hypervigilance is often seen in trauma. Babette Rothschild explains bodily symptoms that emerge with this kind of hypervigilance are "accelerated heart rate, cold sweating, rapid breathing, heart palpitations, hypervigilance, and hyperstartle response (jumpiness). When chronic these symptoms can lead to sleep disturbances, loss of appetite, sexual dysfunction, and difficulties in concentrating."[8]

FIGHT, FLIGHT, OR FREEZE

Harvard psychologist Kaethe Weingarten explains:

> When a person is repeatedly exposed to threat or is exposed to an extreme threat, the LC actually changes: it becomes hyperresponsive to stress signals.

This produces the felt experience of hypervigilance for the individual.... Under usual conditions of stress the body prepares for fight or flight, and when the threat is past (the threat ends or the person successfully fights or gets away), the reaction subsides. However, if the threat is extreme and the brain perceives that neither fight nor flight can succeed, the body may go into a freeze response.[9]

Under these conditions, "the sympathetic and the parasympathetic, function simultaneously." Weingarten continues:

This has been likened to pushing your foot down on the accelerator and the brakes of a car at the same time. Attention is narrowed and heightened. The limbs go limp; the body and mind feel numb; the person "goes dead" like a possum or mouse. This reaction cannot be consciously willed or chosen it happens to us.[10]

Those who have experienced some form of sexual abuse where their flight or fight responses were unsuccessful may be more likely to find themselves in freeze mode in the presence of their abuser or a new abuser. I have spoken to a number of young women who have expressed great amounts of shame and guilt because they believed that the third, fourth, or fifth time they were abused, they just "let it happen." She might say something like, "I could have called for help. I could have tried to push away, but it was like my mind just went numb." One young woman explained that she is beginning to "doubt and wonder" if she "was to blame . . . because this abuse just seems to keep happening, but with different people and because I am the remaining factor that does not change, then I must be the problem."[11] And here we see, how the brain's physiology might condition one to be more easily susceptible to cycles of abuse and shame. After years and years of abuse, a young woman who freezes subconsciously comes to the conclusion that neither fighting nor fleeing will make any difference to her situation. So when abuse threatens to emerge now, her brain is programmed to go into this freeze mode where she simply shuts down. This might make sense from a biological point of view, but you can see just how easily a victim might come to the conclusion that she is compliant in the abuse.

TRAUMA AND TRIGGERS

It is difficult to adequately describe the symptoms of post-traumatic stress without actually having experienced it. The neurophysiological symptoms listed above (accelerated heart rate, cold sweat, jumpiness, etc.) often come about due to *triggers*, or those events that set off the alarm bells in the amygdala. This trigger prompts a seemingly inappropriately elevated response to the stimuli.

If you have ever found yourself on the verge of falling asleep and then unexpectedly get jolted awake with the sensation of falling, then you might have a small understanding of what it's like to experience this kind of physiological trigger-like response. Some will report similar jolts to alertness ten times a day at random moments.

There have been conversations regarding "trigger warnings" in various settings—academic settings in particular. Some argue that these kinds of alerts are not only unnecessary but are actually harmful in that they coddle students and are not preparing them for the "real world." While it is impossible to anticipate every trigger for a particular group of people, there are some topics that are more prone to triggers than others. I give my students warning when speaking about highly sensitive topics. I alert my students when we will be discussing sexual assault or abuse. When we are anticipating conversations regarding disturbing racial discrimination, I will let my students know in advance. Not in order to give my students an opportunity to skip class, but to encourage my students—those who have experienced pain and those who have not—to be mindful and bring their best selves to class. My hope is that when a student knows we are dealing with a highly charged topic, they will act differently. And so the young woman who has experienced sexual assault can come to class ready—perhaps with an icy cold drink she can clutch, acting as a grounding object, keeping her present to her surroundings. Perhaps she will enter class with a tin of mints or something to fiddle with. Maybe she will enter the classroom repeating particular phrases she finds empowering and encouraging. Perhaps she'll have begun her morning with prayer and meditation in an effort to attend class with a gently held heart and spirit. And maybe she's even planned for to meet a safe friend for lunch following the class.

The trigger warnings are not just for the students who have experienced trauma. They also serve a purpose for those students who have not experienced trauma. The hope is that all students would attend with a heightened desire to listen and speak thoughtfully. In short, I use trigger warnings with the hope that my students will attend class with their best selves ready to engage.

JACOB GOES TO SCHOOL

The school year was beginning, and Sarah contacted Jacob's teacher to explain his situation and to ask to be alerted prior to any fire drills so she could remove Jacob from class. Jacob's teacher described an anxious little boy who was continually running to the door to be first in line anytime the class had to go somewhere. He wanted to be near the teacher without any danger of getting left behind. Likewise, on the playground, the normally energetic and imaginative little boy stayed close to his teacher's side.

Eventually Jacob dropped down to one counseling appointment a week, and after some extended time, he slowly came back to the boy he was prior to the accident. Sarah felt like things had mostly gotten back to normal by December. Sarah describes a school assignment where the children in Jacob's class were instructed to color a gingerbread house. Jacob's was a beautifully colored gingerbread house—with flames shooting off the roof and smoke billowing up in the air. Sarah asked Jacob about his drawing and he responded with a simple, "Duh, Mom. The gingerbread house is on fire." The smoke was no longer crippling; instead it was simply a storyline Jacob could draw from when he was so inclined.

TRAUMA AND TESTIMONY

There is much to be drawn from Sarah's story. Where I want to focus, however, are those places where Sarah discusses the tension of hiding her story and sharing her story. While Sarah experienced a great deal of angst watching the struggles her son endured, there was also the fear and the shame surrounding *where* and *how* to talk about these struggles.

She found her own frustration rising while considering the lack of attention PTSD received in her medical communities:

> In the medical community, I go to a lot of educational things and a lot of times when I've gone to presentations about children and trauma they focus a lot on the medical issues, and then there might be one or two slides about how kids would be susceptible to PTSD, and then they just move on as if it can't be a huge component of the story. So, I just thought that was interesting that even the medical community just kind of glazes over it like it's not really a big deal.
>
> I remember feeling, when we had gotten through the hospitalization that we were good and golden, and everything was great, when really we hadn't even hit the hardest part in this whole road. I thought being in the hospital and finding out your kid has a skull fracture or even seeing your kid trampled by a horse was the worst thing we could go through, when honestly it was yet to come and we had no idea. The PTSD is what ended up being life-altering for us. And so I just want to stand up and shout at these programs and say, "Hey! Why don't we talk about this more? This is a big deal!"

Sarah readily acknowledges conversations concerning trauma to be "a big deal." Nevertheless, in the midst of her own story, she found herself holding back from sharing her story with others.

> I felt like I didn't have anybody to talk to about it. Because how many other friends do you have whose kids think that someone is going to shoot him? And

> I was afraid if I told my mom-friends, they'd think my kid was weird and not want their kids around Jacob. I felt like I'd be judged, "You must let your kids watch terrible things."

There were multiple fears in play for Sarah: fears she would be judged as a bad mom who exposes her children to violent television shows. Fears that Jacob's friends would pull away if they knew of his struggles. Furthermore, Sarah wondered what good it would do to share their experiences anyway.

> I was scared to share with people. And I think too that the times I wanted to share it, I put myself in my friends' shoes and thought, "What if somebody was telling me about this about their kid? What would I say?" I feel like I'd have no words to help them. I thought, "We sound like we're completely crazy." I was afraid to tell people what we were living because it was (1) very scary and (2) very dark. I didn't feel like people would understand. And it was a time when I felt very alone. I had great family support because my mom and David's mom and dad were very supportive of us as parents and saying that we were doing the right thing and we needed to get him help and that it would be okay. But I was scared to tell other people.

Additionally, there was also the concern that it might be inappropriate to share such private things within her son's life. What did respecting Jacob's privacy look like? "I didn't want to put Jacob's personal mental health issues out on the internet. Everybody loves to share things on Facebook and social media, and I didn't want to do that for my son. I didn't want to put him out for the world like that," Sarah explained.

CONCLUSION

Sarah is somewhat guarded in the ways in which she speaks of their experience. "People always say that things happen for a reason," she explains, "And I don't know if I believe that all the time. Like maybe sometimes life is just hard. Like if you lost your baby, I don't know the reason for that. Maybe sometimes bad things just happen. But it was really redeeming to see how we went through all this with Jacob."

In the years following Jacob's experience with trauma therapy, Sarah found herself an unexpected advocate for trauma therapy, gently reaching out to people in the community who might be searching for this kind of help. This would include sharing her experience with EMDR with Karen a few short years later. We will look at Karen's story in the chapter that follows.

NOTES

1. Names have been changed.
2. Sarah. Interview by Amanda Hontz Drury. Digital recording. Marion, IN. May 20, 2016. All subsequent quotations are from Sarah.
3. Jones, *Trauma and Grace*, 13.
4. Jones, *Trauma and Grace*, 14.
5. Felicia C. Snell is a licensed therapist in Indianapolis, Indiana.
6. EMDR (Eye Movement Desensitization and Reprocessing) is a psychotherapy technique that involves engaging in both hemispheres of the brain while an individual simultaneously articulates a traumatic event.
7. Rothschild, *The Body Remembers*, 6.
8. Rothschild, *Remembers*, 7.
9. Kaethe Weingarten, *Common Shock: Witnessing Violence Every Day* (New York: Dutton, 2003), 44.
10. Weingarten, *Common Shock*, 44.
11. Woman 1, interviewed by Amanda Hontz Drury. Written Interview. Marion, Indiana. February 2014.

Theological Interlude 3

Jesus Weeps

Perhaps one of the greatest tensions of the Christian life is knowing how to balance the suffering of today with the hope for tomorrow. This is, perhaps, most clearly seen at funerals. On one side of the spectrum is utter and complete despair. A kind of grief without hope. At the other extreme is the seemingly out-of-place smile with the declaration of "better places." One has no hope for life after death. The other refuses to acknowledge the pain of this world. What does it look like to intermingle pain and hope? To dwell in the middle?

In the eleventh chapter of John's gospel, Jesus travels to Bethany where his friend Lazarus has just died. While it is a short trip from Jerusalem to Bethany, Jesus lingers in his travels, arriving three days after Lazarus has died. When Jesus arrives at the tomb, he's greeted rather accusingly by Lazarus's sisters, and then he cries. He weeps. It is ironic how the shortest verse in the Bible seems to be the longest part of life. Weeping.

We know what happens next—Jesus commands the friends to roll away the stone and then calls out in a loud voice: "Lazarus, come forth!" The dead man emerges from the grave wrapped in strips of linen. His grave clothes are removed, and he is handed back to his family.

One of the things that strikes me about this passage is the fact that Jesus *knew* Lazarus would be raised to life. He told his disciples, "This sickness will not end in death." Jesus walked to Bethany *knowing* Lazarus would be fine. Yet despite this hope, despite this knowledge, Jesus nevertheless chooses to be present to the pain of the moment and weep. And all who witness this scene testify to the love Jesus has for his friend.

If I were the Son of God I would have rushed into the city proclaiming what was to come. I'd have entered shouting: "Don't cry! Everything's going to be okay. Just hold on a bit longer!" My hope—my knowledge of what was to come would preempt whatever was already taking place at the tomb. I would leave no room for tears—what's the point of tears when joy is about to commence?

What we see Jesus do, however, is create space in the middle for despairing hope. Or hopeful despair. With full confidence in what is to come, Jesus pauses in the middle and weeps. And this is our invitation as well. To stand in the middle, intermingling grief and hope with tears streaming down our cheeks.

Chapter 4

Articulation

Karen's Story

One of my greatest fears in writing this book was that I would commodify other people's pain or steal their stories. This is one of the reasons why I gave those I interviewed the opportunity to read their chapters before I sent them to my editor.

Karen read her chapter before anyone else set eyes on it. Karen had lost her husband in traumatic circumstances and graciously agreed to meet with me to chronicle some of her journey over the span of three years. As painful as these conversations were, I wish I could somehow articulate the beauty and laughter that emerged simultaneously with the grief.

Soon after sending a full draft to Karen she contacted me in order to say that while every word I had written was true, it wasn't the full story. Her story had continued to evolve after our last interview, and she wanted it included in the chapter to give a fuller account of her experience.

We arranged to meet again, and over coffee, Karen told me: "I will miss Ross every day for the rest of my life." But, she added, she has hope. Yes, there is pain, but that pain is intermingled with hope.[1]

I was afraid to write about hope in this chapter. I was worried that any talk of hope or healing would somehow undermine her pain or dishonor the memory of Ross. I was afraid the deep moments of healing that Karen experienced would be used by well-intended others to pressure grieving friends toward a similar end. I didn't want Karen's words of hope to be turned into platitudes that could be lobbed at others. The moment testimonies are turned into instruction manuals, they go from being balms to poison. I also didn't want it to seem as if I was tagging on a tidy ending to a painful story. But telling Karen's story honestly means not only giving painful snapshots into her grief but also chronicling her journey through the haze of pain to a place of hope. And so my desire is that Karen's story will be told in such a way that her despair is not devoid of hope and that the hope she experiences will take despair seriously.

Karen did not haphazardly stumble upon this hope; rather, it has emerged after painful admissions, declarations, and questions. While she has struggled her way into this hope, it is hope nonetheless. In other words, she has wrestled with the angel of the Lord; and while she is walking away with a limp, a new day has begun. This is her story.

THE EVENT

On August 14, 2013, Ross and Karen were working in their backyard. Karen was mowing the lawn, and Ross was digging a trench in hopes of solving the problem of a flooding basement. While digging in the trench, the sides collapsed, instantly trapping Ross. Fifty-five-year-old Ross was buried up to his neck, with the compacted clay making it impossible to breathe.

Ross's wife, Karen, was a witness to this trauma. She had been mowing the yard when the accident occurred and immediately jumped into the ditch to try to save her husband, frantically attempting to move the clay to get air into his lungs. While it was mere minutes before first responders arrived, they were ultimately unable to revive Ross. It took emergency responders between 30 and 45 minutes to dig Ross out of the trench. The dirt was so compacted that even though Karen was using her hands to dig, by the time she got to the hospital she says she didn't have a speck of dirt on her hands or her shoes.

News of the accident spread quickly, and while Ross was in the emergency room, over fifty friends and community members gathered in the hospital waiting room praying and awaiting news. Doctors worked tirelessly, hoping something could be done, but it was clear he was gone. Soon after, Karen began the wrenching task of contacting her children who were literally around the world to share with them the news.

As one might imagine, there are many details that could be included in this story, but suffice it to say, there was a tragic accident resulting in the death of a beloved husband, father, and friend. Ross owned a business in town and was known for offering stable jobs to ex-convicts. The entire community was stricken.

Karen would later explain that on that day in August 2013, it seemed as if her life ended as well. She speaks of a "strong feeling that this isn't my life. This is someone else's. This is not what we worked hard for or dreamed of. Not what we planned on.... And now I have this life that is not my life."[2]

In the days that followed the accident, Karen awoke each morning with a sense of panic. "I was desperate," she said, "Just full of fear. I would wake up in the morning in this horrible state of just feeling like I was dying, and I didn't know how I was going to survive." The fear, Karen said, was the worst thing she had ever felt in her life. She explained to her pastor: "I will learn to live without my husband. I will learn to live with the grief. And I will handle whatever financial ruin or emotional devastation might come. But I will not live like this. I won't hang around for this feeling of fear and anxiety and sleeplessness and depression. I knew that I wasn't going to get through it if I didn't do something." Psychoanalyst Donald Winnicott speaks to this fear, explaining that oftentimes that which we fear has already happened, the logic being that we project into the future the trauma from our past.[3]

Part of this fear was the realization that all bets are off, and there are no guarantees. Her husband is gone, who's to say her children aren't next? There is a terror that comes with trauma. It's like looking into a black hole and realizing the darkness is even deeper than originally thought.

We learn our colors young. Most three-year-olds can identify the color black. As we grow and our understandings become more nuanced, some of us might notice various undertones of greens or purples. We know black. And then someone introduces us to "Vanta Black." Vanta Black is made up of carbon nanotubes and is currently the darkest material known on earth, absorbing 99.965 percent of all light. I didn't know how dark dark could be until I saw Vanta Black. It's disorienting. You look at this color and feel dizzy—like you're falling. Artist Anish Kapoor who works with this color says, "Imagine a space that's so dark that as you walk in you lose all sense of where you are, what you are, and especially all sense of time."[4] You think you've had a dark night of the soul in the past, and then you experience Vanta Black, and you realize that was more like dusk than night. And there exists the fear: "What if this gets worse?" When I reach a Vanta Black place in life, there is the crippling terror that perhaps there is a darkness darker than Vanta Black. That perhaps tomorrow a new color will be manufactured that absorbs 99.966 percent of light. And the fear is crippling.

Years following her husband's death, Karen walked alongside her daughter, Meredith, through a high-risk pregnancy. She explains: "We were afraid that we were going to lose the baby and maybe Meredith, and all through that, I remember thinking, 'I have paid my dues, served my time, you can't do this!' But knowing that God absolutely could. . ." Karen's voice trailed off before she continued to speak, "I kept thinking, 'I don't get life. I don't get you Lord. I don't get how this works. I just don't get it.'"[5]

A few days after the funeral Karen met up with Sarah who shared with her the trauma therapy their son Jacob had received years earlier. Karen decided to place a call to Felicia.

> Being a nurse, I'm skeptical by nature. I keep my feet firmly planted on the ground. But I was feeling desperate enough that I was going to believe in this

[therapy] no matter what. Plus, I did a lot of research ahead of time. I started reading about EMDR. . . . The thing that appealed to me . . . was that I could read the pathophysiology and [understand] what was actually happening. There was a good biological explanation of how it worked, and that made sense to me.

Karen describes her first encounter with Felicia: "I talked with her for a while and said, 'What should I plan this to be like?' And she said, 'You'll probably feel better after the first session. It'll go away; it won't last. But you'll feel better for a day. And you'll be exhausted.' And she was exactly right. I was totally spent."

Karen speaks of that first year feeling foggy. As if her neurons weren't firing as fast as they should and her perceptions were somewhat blunted.

I was in a stupor. I was just so stunned. My whole life changed in an instant, and I can't say that strongly enough. I mean literally it felt like I died that same day. It felt like the world was a completely different place. It even *looked* like a completely different place to me . . . I mean literally there would be something in front of me on my desk at home, and I'd take the whole house apart looking for it and the next day, there it was right in front of my eyeballs on the desk. . . . You're trying to deal with finances, insurances, and in my case, autopsy reports and visits from people. And you know that this is important stuff that you have to pay attention to, but I couldn't tell which end was up. I could not read. People gave me grief books, but I couldn't focus. Until just recently, probably two or three months ago, I hadn't read a book clear through at all. I just couldn't focus.

Karen found herself losing a great deal of weight that first year. She was vomiting every morning and terrified that she would be reduced to a "psychological cripple that was going to end up in an institution somewhere." Her experience with EMDR left her with the hope that perhaps it was possible to make the unbearable pain more tolerable—if even just a little.

That hope began to emerge in the form of a camera and very practical advice from Felicia. Karen was instructed to "take pictures" of anything that she felt unable to clean out or sort through, so as to keep it from being completely lost to her. "That was huge for me," Karen said. Felicia instructed Karen to not begin by moving things in her husband's vanity. The items on his vanity, Felicia explained, would involve other senses, triggering a more emotional response. "Start with his clothing," Felicia said. Karen followed her advice, taking two or three items of clothing out of the closet at a time. Every time she removed something from the closet, she put something in its place. "Don't leave empty spaces that can mock you," Felicia had told her.

After the clothes, Karen moved to Ross's vanity, camera in hand.

> I have pictures of dirty old shoes and the boots he had on in the trench. And I have pictures of his toothbrush and the brush he brushed his hair with. And I don't go back and look at them, but I have them. [Felicia told me to] "Take something that smells like him and vacuum seal it." I put a t-shirt of his through my food saver. And I've never opened it, but I can if I want to. I took a bottle of aftershave, because that's what he always smelled like. I have it sealed up so I can smell it if they stop making it.

Felicia also walked Karen through what she could do when she became weary of well-intended hugs: "I'm a hugger, but it got to be that I couldn't walk across campus without getting six hugs on the sidewalk." Felicia had Karen stand and said, "I'm going to give you a hug. What are you going to do?"

"Probably hug you back," Karen replied.

"No," Felicia said and physically walked her through the process of taking hold of the other person's arms, gently bringing them down, and saying, "Thank you so much for caring." And then, Felicia said, "just hold their hands . . . and talk to them." Simple habits like this helped Karen feel as if she could take back a small amount of control in her life.

One of the places where the trauma manifested itself in Karen's life was in her driving. Felicia's office was an hour and a half from her house, and Karen became afraid of her new driving habits.

> I would find myself screeching my brakes right on someone's tail. Or getting lost, I can't tell you how many times I got lost right in my hometown. Just totally disoriented about where I was or where I was headed. And [Felicia] said, "Quit listening to NPR when you're driving. Put on some really horrible rap or rock music, something you hate. Something that you're going to have to think about. Take a piece of Velcro and stick it to your steering wheel, and run your fingers over it. Something that's going to stimulate other senses. It will help you focus. Get a glass of iced tea or something cold or something bitter. Don't get something you really love, get something you don't really love the taste of or haven't tasted before. Keep it in your car, and drink that."

While the trauma therapy did not remove the intense grief, it allowed Karen to function again. The paralyzing fear slowly gave way to a deep sadness. Her grief was an intense burden to bear, but she was no longer being crushed under the weight of it.

THE SEARCH FOR SUCCESSFUL GRIEVING AND "COMPASSIONATE OTHERS"

With much of the first year spent absorbed in the details of her husband's former business, properties, and so on, Karen claims she didn't really begin to fully grieve until the second year. People had told her that the second year would be worse than the first, but that once she went through the second year she would find things getting better. But she didn't. And having subconsciously set a two-year timeline in her brain, Karen was distressed to come to the end of two years and still find herself in the throes of deep grief. She began experiencing anxiety on *how* she grieved. "Something really is wrong with me. I'm doing this wrong." She turned to a friend with the question:

"What do I do? What do I do to get through this successfully?"

"Karen," came her friend Judy's reply, "You are pathologically desiring to do this right, and there isn't a right way to do this." Friends like Judy were integral to Karen in her grief journey. One friend watched movies with her on Friday evenings. Another arranged regular lunch dates with Karen to keep her eating. There were calls, and cards, and invitations. The recognition Karen experienced from dear friends was indispensable. Pastoral theologian Deborah van Deusen Hunsinger might describe these friends as "caring others."[6] Hunsinger explains:

> Healing begins as the traumatized begin to piece together a coherent narrative, creating a web of meaning around unspeakable events while remaining fully connected emotionally both to themselves and to their listener. It takes courage even to begin such a conversation. Their feelings can be confusing and difficult to sort out. Often there seem to be no words that adequately describe the horror. Moreover, is it safe to trust the listener? Feelings of shame, fear of judgment, extreme vulnerability are common.[7]

This experience of voicing "the terror and helplessness, the sense of moral outrage and personal violation, the sorrow, hurt, anger, and grief—becomes the essential first step in piecing together a coherent narrative," Hunsinger continues.[8] The ability to voice these kinds of experiences must happen in the "lively presence of a caring other." Bearing witness as a "caring other" is not a simple task:

> Who can bear the anguish of such a narrative, without minimizing or denying it, without giving advice or offering strategies to overcome it? Who can listen without offering empty platitudes or switching the story to a similar story of his own? Who has the wisdom to refrain from asking intrusive questions prompted by his own anxiety, allowing the traumatized person space to tell his story his

own way at his own pace? Who can offer a compassionate, caring presence, free of pity or sympathy, free of judgment, praise, or blame?[9]

Caring others are not those who simply elicit testimony from others. In fact, sometimes bearing witness as a caring other means slowing down a conversation. Hunsinger explains at length:

> Talking about it can, in fact, make matters worse. Any kind of direct processing of the traumatic experience needs to be balanced at all times with a sense of safety and containment. Anchoring oneself in the present, feeling safe with one's listener, processing one small piece at a time, mourning each of the profound losses involved—all these steps take time, patience, and exquisite self-care. Trauma specialists are trained to pay attention to signs of distress and deliberately slow down the process, remembering the maxim that "the slower you go, the faster you get there." The goal in talking about it is to stay fully connected to the feelings without becoming overwhelmed. Eye contact with the caregiver, slowing down the pace, taking a break from the past, returning to the present with clear focus on one's bodily sensations—all help to put on the brakes. Understanding what is happening and why profoundly assists the healing process as well. This is why a clear conceptual understanding of trauma is important: understanding becomes a part of the holding environment that contains anxiety and increases a sense of empowerment.[10]

"The slower you go, the sooner you get there." Part of being a caring other is to attempt to discern the regulation and pacing of painful conversations. Hunsinger also refers to these caring others as compassionate witnesses. This kind of recognition of testimony, she explains, "does not remove the pain of trauma, it reconfigures it by restoring human connection, building strength and hope even in the midst of tragedy."[11]

Recognition for Karen took place both in thoughtful conversation with compassionate others and in thoughtful actions. Small groups from her church came and finished the drainage project Ross had started. Facility Services from Indiana Wesleyan University and young men Ross had mentored arranged to care for the acres and acres of land.

The ditch where Ross had died had been filled in, and there was a giant mound of dirt in its place. Karen was told that in a year or so the dirt would settle in naturally and the mound would no longer be there. But this meant Karen could not look at her backyard without her eyes being drawn to the makeshift memorial of dirt where her husband died. When church friends learned of this mound, they decided to work the land until it lay flat and then seed the area so it once again blended into the landscape. They could not speed up the timetable of grief, but they could flatten the earth faster than what would naturally occur.

Chapter 4

THE UNRECOGNIZED SELF

Of course, it's much easier to fill a trench in the ground than it is to fill the emptiness caused by grief. Especially jarring for Karen was the realization that she no longer recognized herself. The person she thought she was disintegrated in the face of trauma. The kind of Christian she thought she was prior to the accident was elusive.

> I thought I would be the person that [would say], "Yes it was really hard, but I had victory in Jesus." And "I had all the strength of the power of God behind me in this," and I should be that person that said, "Yes, weeping has lasted for a night but joy comes in the morning." Or, you know, "The Lord will never leave me nor forsake me."

Karen wondered if her inability to claim these promises was a failure on her part. And she feared that anyone who called this less than a failure was "just making excuses for me."

Throughout our interview, Karen kept coming back to this mental place where she thought she should be. But it is the "shoulds" that hinder healing. These "shoulds" keep us in the past and distract us from focusing on the present. Karen's "shoulds" were exacerbated by one-dimensional understandings of faith. "If you've grown up in the church," Karen continued,

> and you've watched people who have shown that face of victory in Jesus, you think *What is wrong with me? This isn't that bad! I should be doing better.* I probably say that to myself every day. I should be doing better. There's something that should have changed faster . . . I especially looked to the people who had it all together spiritually, and I'd beat myself up for having all the questions and not saying the right things to everybody. I want to be the person who they invite up into the pulpit to share victory. But I'm not. I have victory; I certainly do. But I'm not going to stand there and say, "Jesus is enough"—as if that's going to solve everything right now.

Certainly, there were times when it could have been easier for her to settle for less than authentic recognition. "I have wished that I could just quote the promises of God. But," she says, "I'm not a person who can glibly claim promises when I don't know what they mean anymore . . . I'm not the person who can say I'm fine and leave it there . . . I don't know if I'm just a poor Christian, or if it's just telling the truth."

Nevertheless, she is grateful for what she *can* say. "I'm okay," she says. "I'm okay. I'm upright. I'm talking. Walking. And I'm not in the fetal position somewhere . . . I give myself a lot of credit for not slumping into alcoholism or addiction . . . I think I get credit for that. Somedays that's all I give myself." Sometimes Karen will simply say "I'm fine," or "I'm okay," not because that's necessarily how she feels, but because they serve as prophetic words of hope in order to, as she says, "take the next breath." In fact, Karen got into the habit of saying these words regularly: "I have started saying to myself, 'I'm okay. I'm not alone. I'm not scared. I'm capable. And I'm enough.' And I repeat those to myself and keep them written on my laptop because it's taken me a very long time to actually believe it."

RECOGNIZING HERSELF IN OTHERS

While Karen was unrecognizable to herself, she began looking for fragments of herself in the stories of others. She took in testimonies of trauma from others to see if she might catch a glimpse of herself. This was a practice that was both frustrating and rewarding. It was frustrating, she explained, to watch someone else go through the grief process in a way in which she didn't understand. "You look for other people with traumas of their own . . . I would search for some kind of recognition in their grief," she explained, "But [their] experience was just so totally different from mine that there wasn't any recognition. It made me crazy!" Much of Karen's experience was reminiscent of Tolstoy's opening line in *Anna Karenina*: "All happy families are alike; each unhappy family is unhappy in its own way."[12]

With that said, Karen has experienced profound moments of recognition during some of her interactions with others who have experienced trauma. There are people, she says, that just "get grief." Their understanding of grief melds with her own. Karen describes going to a funeral home and catching the eye of a friend who had experienced trauma. "We see each other in line," Karen says, "and he comes up to me and says, 'We know this, don't we?'" They recognize one another in the midst of sorrow. When she asks a friend how he's doing after losing his wife in an accident, the man simply responds: "Well, you know." Karen continues: "And I'm like, 'I get it,' but that's all I got. I get it but I don't know how to make it better for him. There's not a thing I can do or that I'd even want to say to try and make it better."

Oftentimes, however, the recognition is not even articulated. Karen describes moments at church or elsewhere where she catches the eye of a fellow griever, and they simply hold the gaze for a brief pause in time, silently bearing witness to the trauma. "The wonderful thing about somebody who has experienced loss is that they are an eye you can catch and see that somebody else gets this. I'm not alone in this. . . . There are just people like that," Karen explains.

Karen acknowledges that one does not have to experience the trauma of loss in order to "get her." She acknowledges the friends in her life that perhaps didn't "get it" at first but listened and kept on listening until eventually "they got it." This requires remarkable courage on behalf of her friends. The only way to avoid the risk of saying the wrong thing is by saying nothing at all. Karen was surrounded by dear friends who kept taking risks and reaching out until they were able to recognize Karen in her grief. She speaks of emails from friends that come throughout the year. Emails with memories or simple statements like "I miss Ross every day." "And that means the world to me—that I'm not the only person that remembers that he's not here and that he hasn't just passed into history in everybody's experience because he surely hasn't in ours," Karen says.

Karen tells the story of a friend who called her up and asked if he could come over to her office simply to talk about Ross. "And he drove over and walked clear back to my office. By the time he got back to my office, there were tears in his eyes and coming down his face, and he just told me a couple of stories about his last interactions with Ross, and we both cried, and it was the most wonderful blessing to me. It was so important," Karen recalls.

Of course, there were less than helpful moments in her relationships with acquaintances. Karen describes the conversations that began with, "At least," as in, "At least your husband is in heaven," or, "At least you have a busy job so that when you go home at night you have things to do or things to think about." There were other well-intended platitudes, as is often the case when there is trauma in a Christian community. "They think they're trying to help you," Karen explains insightfully, "but what they are really doing is reassuring themselves that you're okay so that they don't have to worry about you." And this is where Karen musters immense grace for others: "I realized the people who said things that weren't very helpful were all grieving, too. They were grieving themselves. . . . And they just needed love."

THE EXPIRATION OF ARTICULATION

Even with the meaningful recognition she received from friends, Karen continually danced around the question of whether or not she is grieving properly. She is aware of the fact that she is stuck on the simple statement, "I miss Ross." But how often can you make a statement of that sort? It's already been said. What do you say when you've already said all the words there are to say? What do you say when the words you want to speak are words that you've already spoken over and over again? Is there an expiration date on speaking of trauma? Is Karen allowed to say "I miss Ross," over and over and over again? How many times is Karen allowed to speak of her grief? Karen voices her hesitations to speak of her husband. "You get really tired of being that girl . . . I don't want to be a burden on other people. You know, people having this sense of, 'Goodness! Does she have to talk about Ross in every conversation?' Because I can," Karen gently laughs, "I can bring Ross into every conversation within four seconds."

Perhaps the unspoken expiration date of talking about Ross could be lifted by other's broaching the subject. Of course, that would require people having the courage to initiate conversations about Ross. I remember being reluctant to do so. The first few times I initiated a conversation about Ross I began by saying, "Karen, I don't want to make you cry." Karen would always cut me off with a smile and say something along the lines of "I'm always two seconds away from tears. They are going to come anyway and I'd rather they come while we're talking about Ross." Karen acknowledges both the joy and pain that come with talking about Ross. Her experience sounds similar to C. S. Lewis in *A Grief Observed*: "It doesn't really matter whether you grip the arms of the dentist's chair or let your hands lie in your lap. The drill drills on."[13]

What if we met pain with the same profundity we ascribe to love? We do not grow weary of stating our love. Repetitive declarations of love are often appreciated; in fact, we may look down upon those who say something like, "I told you I loved you on our wedding day. I'll let you know if something changes." What if the church treated trauma in the same way we treated love? What if there's value in saying it over and over again without a particular goal in mind. It just is. What if we created space for Karen to say, "I miss Ross," every single day of her life if she so chooses without worrying about whether or not her sentiments have expired? What if statements like "I miss Ross" were met with gentle questions: "What do you miss about him?" "How is missing Ross today different than it was a year ago?" "Is it different in the morning? At night?" "What do you notice about missing him? His laugh? His smell?" Curious and compassionate listening can be an act of love for the one bearing the pain.

This theory of articulation does not function like a board game where you move from spot to spot until you reach the end and the game is over. Moving from Event to Articulation to Recognition does not conclude the experience. Karen does not share her story once and then move on. Rather she returns to articulation over and over again—as many times as she desires, even if it's a journey she grows weary of. As stated earlier, the experience one has moving through this theory of articulation then becomes a new experience of itself. And each one of these new events shapes how Karen sees herself and relates to the world.

We have a number of phrases in the English language that aim for the resolution of difficulties. Phrases like "Get over it," "Move on," "Rise above it," "Overcome," "Pull yourself together"—all of these phrases have connotations of movement, as if the point is to move from one place to another. Phrases like this, Karen explains, have an "onerous of blame—as though I alone control it all and if I would just 'Buck up' all would be well." But recognition does not have a destination—a Theory of Articulation is a cycle—there is no conclusion to the process. Articulation here becomes less of a means to an end, and more of an invitation to share space.

It would be a misnomer to say that Karen does not have a support system of people who love her. She speaks of "knowing that people were on my side and no matter how hard it was, people were grieving with me and wanted to help make it better. Or to just sit quietly by and just be with you. The people were with me in this, and were on my side." But again, we come back to Butler's words reminding us of the impossibility of fully sharing our stories, and we acknowledge that there are places on the path of grief that Karen walks alone regardless of who is next to her.

THE ARTICULATION OF OTHERS

It's not only that Karen wants to talk about Ross but also that she wants to hear others talk about Ross. "One of the things that almost immediately was so hard for me was this sense that time was passing and Ross wasn't in it. And he was being relegated to history . . . to people's memories." Karen knows that stories and memories were shared at Ross's funeral, but she readily admits she doesn't remember any of it. "You're in it all alone there at first. You really are. I don't care who's around you, you're in it all alone there and you . . . never get to hear—I don't get to talk to the people who were at the funeral about the service." Karen gave a short laugh as she added, "No one wants to talk to you about your husband's funeral."

It was about this time in our interview when Karen leaned forward and made a confession. She worried about sounding morbid, but confessed that she wanted to hear from other people what it was like for them to hear the devastating news of her husband's death. I received her words and took a deep and anxious breath and asked Karen if she wanted to hear my experience. She quickly stated she did.

I was anxious sharing my story with Karen. I was afraid it would sound like I was trying to garner sympathy from her. She was the one with the loss, so it seemed like she should be the one that was sharing. But the kind of recognition that Karen desired at that moment was for others to articulate their experiences with this devastating event.

I told Karen my story about being in my bed around 10:30 pm and seeing cryptic comments on social media that seemed to indicate some sort of communal tragedy. People I knew quite well were indicating heartbreak of some sort. I don't remember what I Googled, but I went on an internet search and found a breaking story with the headline, "Local Man Killed in Accident." Knowing I likely had a connection to the tragedy given the number of friends who were posting online, I tried to get through the article as quickly as I could to find the name of the deceased. What I found, however, was that I couldn't read. I saw the headline and then found my eyes leaping around the screen looking for information all without actually reading any words. My eyes wouldn't move in a straight line. I remember thinking: "One of my friends has died," and spending a considerable amount of time trying to get my eyes to move in a left to right fashion so that I could actually take in the news. After I found Ross's name I remember sitting up wide awake in my bed, hands shaking.

I finished my story and after a long pause, Karen said quietly, "What an awful way to find out. I'm so sorry."

I was struck by Karen's compassion and gentleness. She is the one who lost a husband and here I am complaining about my hands that wouldn't stop shaking. It seemed wrong that I should somehow be receiving sympathy and care from a widow. And yet, this was something Karen wanted to share with me. To experience the intimacy of sharing this painful story.

I asked Karen if she had ever asked anyone else to share their stories from that horrible day. "Not really," she said. "I haven't had the courage and somehow, it feels self-serving. Does that make sense? It feels like asking for you to prove to me how much you loved Ross." Karen laughed, "Like, tell me how awful this was for you." Karen said as she assumed the position of a fascinated, captive audience. "On a scale of one to ten," we joked.

Karen's desire to hear these stories is no different than someone asking, "Where were you when JFK was shot?" or, "What were you doing when the twin towers fell?" There is something very intimate about sharing a common experience. We ask questions about 9/11 not because we are trying to ascertain new facts about that horrific day, but because we are looking for an intimate connection with the person right in front of us. "There's a memorialization too," Karen said, "repeating your story turns it into reality." Even though the stories told are from the past, they serve as a way of grounding Karen to her present circumstances. Her husband's passing was not a vague blimp on people's minds, she had witnesses to the devastation of this event.

When my husband John teaches New Testament Survey with undergraduates, he opens the class by dividing them into four teams. He then gives them the task of creating a short news story on what took place on 9/11. They break into their teams, make their lists, and then present to the class. It's fascinating to see how they relay information. Sometimes the information matches; other times, it contradicts each other. Some stories were shared by all four groups;

sometimes, a single group would be responsible for reporting on a lone fact. Their styles are different, too. Some are short and choppy, while others arranged their reports as a kind of lament. This short exercise is what kicks off the unit on the Gospels, illustrating the idea that one event could be looked at from four different perspectives and that when we hold those narratives in tension with one another we have a richer understanding of the life of Jesus.

When Karen hears others' experiences of the day of Ross's death, she's not being morbid; she's looking for a fuller and broader view of what took place. She is seeking confirmation that this was a devastating and disorienting event. Not because she wants to see her friends suffer, but because she desires the intimacy that comes when loved ones hold vigil alongside each other.

Partway through the writing of this chapter Karen asked me how this book was coming along. I hesitated before giving her the honest answer: "Very slowly. I'm having a hard time writing your story in particular."

"Good!" Karen replied, somewhat gratified by my response. I was afraid Karen would (wrongly) hear my confession as an admission that she was an incoherent mess. She took it, however, as recognition that her story is painfully complex and cannot be captured in a few pages.

Today Karen describes her journey through trauma as three steps forward, two steps back. She is striving, she says, to have valleys not quite as deep or as long as the last one. And she's begun riding horses. There is a horse farm not too far from her that actually combines horseback riding and grief. There are stable hands as well as therapists available at all times. One of the things Karen appreciates about resurrecting this interest is that this was something she did not share with Ross. Karen rode horses as a child, but it was not a part of her relationship with Ross. It is, for her, a symbol of her movement forward—she is doing something she loves by herself.

CONCLUSION

The last time Karen and I spoke she shared with me a story of healing that had infused her with hope. Prior to our meeting, Karen was preparing to sell the house she and Ross had built. Another woman who had her own share of pain helped her organize items for a giant garage sale. As the two women worked side by side tagging items the conversation somehow turned to various promises of God. "What does it mean," they asked, "to have that peace that passes understanding? If this is something God is offering, why aren't we experiencing it?" They worked alongside one another mulling over this question.

Soon after, a mother with three young children approached to look at the items for sale. While she perused the wares, her children ran to Karen's backyard and began a noisy game. The mother appeared to be somewhat anxious about her children enjoying themselves in a space where so much pain had transpired. "Does it bother you that the children are so loud?" She asked Karen.

"No!" came Karen's quick reply. "I actually love it!"

"Ah," the woman sighed, "That's the peace that passes understanding," she added, oblivious of Karen's earlier conversation.

Something "clicked" for Karen in that conversation. The realization that she could find joy and delight in the very place where her husband had died did not make sense. But there it was. Life within death. Peace beyond understanding.

NOTES

1. Karen. Interview by Amanda Hontz Drury. Digital recording. Marion, IN. May 25, 2016. Unless otherwise noted, all subsequent quotations are from this interview with Karen.

2. Karen and Rachel. Interview by Amanda Hontz Drury. Digital recording. Marion, IN. August 25, 2016.

3. Donald Winnicott, "Fear of Breakdown," *International Review of Psychoanalysis* 1, (1974): 103–107.

4. "How Black Can Black Be?" *BBC Radio 4's Today Programme*. Transcript, September 23, 2014. http://www.bbc.com/news/entertainment-arts-29326916 accessed August 12, 2016. I'm thankful for conversations with artists Herb Peterson and Graham McClanahan who introduced me to this color.

5. Thankfully, Karen welcomed a healthy granddaughter soon after and since then has welcomed another three grandchildren.

6. Deborah van Deusen Hunsinger, *Bearing the Unbearable: Trauma, Gospel, and Pastoral Care* (Grand Rapids, MI: Eerdmans, 2015), 11. This is a powerful book that deserves careful attention from pastors and all those in helping professions.

7. Hunsinger, *Bearing the Unbearable*, 11.

8. Hunsinger, *Bearing the Unbearable*, 11.

9. Hunsinger, *Bearing the Unbearable*, 11.

10. Hunsinger, *Bearing the Unbearable*, 11–12.

11. Hunsinger, *Bearing the Unbearable*, 25.

12. Leo Tolstoy, *Anna Karenina* (Oxford: Oxford World's Classics, 2016), 3.

13. C. S. Lewis, *A Grief Observed* (New York: Harper One, 1961), 33.

Theological Interlude 4
Clinging to the Dead

Early in the morning on the first day of the week while it was still dark, Mary Magdalene came to the tomb.

—John 20:1

For the past few days, Mary has done nothing but watch. She has been a passive observer. Her attempts to be with Jesus are feeble—perhaps pitiful. She does not have the authority to speak to a religious community condemning a man. She does not have the power to stand up to a government who oversees the execution. So she simply watches, offering nothing but silent witness. She continues her passive witness while he is placed in a tomb. Even the Sabbath laws seem to be working against her. She is kept from attending to the body. The falling of the Sun, marks the impending Sabbath which keeps her from immediately tending to the body. Once again, she is impotent. There is nothing to do. Instead of grieving with her hands, she is left to grieve in passivity. Her hands are still, but her mind is not. Mary does what she can. She cannot save Jesus, but she stands in solidarity with the dying man. She cannot anoint his body on the seventh day of the week, so she waits for the first.

Finally, we come to that first day of the week when Mary is finally empowered to act. She longs to go from silent witness to active mourner. Perhaps her lack of agency these past few days drove her crazy. Perhaps Mary longed for a task—something to do. Perhaps the weight of her passive grief was too strong to wait a moment longer.

And so, on the first day of the week, while it was still dark, Mary acts. She buys. She prepares. She moves. But after maddening, powerless days, Mary arrives at the tomb only to discover there is still nothing for her to do. There is no body. The empty tomb mocks her. There is nothing to busy idle hands.

There is no outlet for her grief. Even her ability to mourn has been stolen from her. Once again, she is stripped of her ability to act. The empty tomb is another indicator of Mary's helplessness—of her complete inability to act.

The empty tomb is not good news for Mary. We forget this sometimes. It eludes our collective memories because we have the ability to step back from the horror with perspective. We proclaim the empty tomb with a glint in our eyes. We know what is coming. Our minds have filled in the empty space of the tomb with deep meaning. We cannot grasp the horror of the barren tomb because our minds have already jumped to a perceived gardener calling our names. The empty tomb for us means hope, assurance, and courage. For Mary Magdalene, however, the empty tomb is despair, trauma, loss upon loss. It's no wonder that with nothing to do, Mary simply turns and flees.

We watch Mary run from the tomb and we long to shout after her: "Hold on a bit longer! It's not what you think! What you were expecting to find is not here, but in its place, you will find something, or someone, that exceeds your greatest hopes."

Perhaps it is during these times in our lives when God seems utterly absent that there exists something that surpasses imagination. We are troubled when we do not see Jesus where we expect to see him. When he is not in the place where we left him. But perhaps it is in that alarming absence where grace breathes.

When we are lost, our father stands at the road waiting for us.
Our shepherd leaves the 99 to search.
Lights are shined, corners are swept,
And when we are found there is a celebration.

So, it is disorienting when the one who finds lost things goes missing.
But perhaps grace breathes when Jesus goes missing.
When Herod misses Jesus, he has already escaped to Egypt.
When his parents miss him, he is teaching in the temple.
When the disciples are without him on the rough sea, Jesus appears on water and calms the storm
When the religious leaders cannot find the man they want to stone, Jesus has already crossed the Jordan
And when the body is gone, Jesus has already risen.
When we go missing, we are lost.
When Jesus goes missing, we are found.
Thanks be to God.

Chapter 5

Recognition
Rachel's Story

Three miles from Karen's house, roughly one year after Ross's death, and three years after Jacob's accident, Rachel experienced a kind of trauma that would serve as a stark before and after point in her life. There are three things to note before we enter into this story. First, it's a difficult story to hear. Second, within this difficult story is a clear sense of hope and healing. Finally, Rachel's path of healing is remarkable, but it does not universally define healing. Rachel's story deserves to be taken as it stands on its own. Similarly, people who share elements of Rachel's narrative should be recognized in their own right without comparing their experiences with Rachel's.

In the early hours of the morning of July 15, an intruder crawled through a first-floor window of Rachel's house. Rachel's husband was spending the week on campus with his doctoral colleagues, and she was left with their four children. The intruder stepped inside of her house and let in two other men through her front door. Hearing the men and fearful for her children, Rachel confronted the intruders who demanded money. She had none to give and begged them not to wake her children. The three men spent the next two hours ransacking the house for valuables and taking turns sexually assaulting her. At one point two of the men filled Rachel's son's backpack with stolen items and took the family van to drive to a nearby convenience store for soda and a bag of chips.[1] The third man remained to continue the assault. Rachel's plea throughout the ordeal was for the safety of her children. After roughly two hours of terror, the men were ready to leave. They threatened to kill the children if Rachel contacted the police. She promised them she would remain quiet. As they left, one of them turned to her and said, "Have a blessed day."[2]

With her phone and computer taken, Rachel had no way of calling for help. She considered walking to a neighbor, but the thought of one of her kids waking up while she was gone was enough to keep her at home. And so, she showered, trying to process what had just taken place. Her daughter did wake up soon after and Rachel laid down with her for a bit, soothing the child back to sleep. She then got up and went to the family room couch.

It was at this point when the gravity of what had taken place began to descend upon her. "I think it felt much scarier," she said.[3] "What just happened?" She wondered. While her children slept, Rachel began to journal. She shared these raw and remarkable words with me and graciously gave permission to include them in this chapter:

July 15, 2014

Oh, Dear Lord hear my prayer. My heart is heavier and more afraid than in my entire life. It is now 5:45 in the morning. 3 hours ago, 3 young men broke into our house, raped me, and stole all our electronics, money, purse, valuables.

Oh Lord thank you sweet Jesus for watching over the children! My insides gush with praise that they remained asleep and safe during the entire event. Thank you. Thank you. Thank you.

But now Lord the fear has come. Fear of his threats to kill the children if I tell anyone. Fear of being in this house knowing that these 3 guys know where I live and where my children sleep. They now have my passwords and pictures . . . Lord please protect our accounts. But I will trust you nonetheless. Our lives were spared. Please never let them come back again. Oh man—and then there's my dear sweet husband. Jesus—he will be so angry, and rightly so. But Lord help him to be understanding and gentle.

Please give me courage. I want to do the right thing. I will call the police. Please give them haste and accuracy and success at finding these men.

And the men. 3 young men making foolish choices. I prayed for them the entire time they were here. Would you please work in their hearts . . . bring them to repentance. Show them Jesus. May their encounter here be one that changed their heart . . . or at least starts a working of the Holy Spirit. I even ask that you'd bring them to confession . . . to returning the items. And Lord, please work so hard in their hearts to stop them from doing anything like this ever again. To me or to anyone.

This was the scariest night of my life.

Lord—I know you were with me while they were here. You gave me strength and not fear. Thank you for your presence.

Please calm my anxious heart. Oh, how quickly it has been pulsing for the last few hours.

And please help me to find truth as I wonder things like:

- *"Jesus, you were here, watching, and you allowed this to happen!?"*
- *"If I said I wouldn't tell anyone, and I feel like I should, how can I live with peace?"*

- *"If you allowed this to happen, and you did, then all I can ask is what good can come out of this? How can I strive harder for you and live fuller in your presence and to your glory?"*

Please order my steps today. My words and interactions.
Please go before me.
Please Lord may I have your blessing.
Lord please give me strength today. I don't know what to tell the children but I have to tell them something so please be my words and my mouth to them. Shine your courage through me. Cover me in Jesus' blood.[4]

Looking back on that night, Rachel explains: "My heart was racing until I started seeing the light. And starting to see the light was the best thing ever. Like, 'Yes! It's the morning. The night's over.'" She continued to journal as the sun began to rise.

Rachel dealt with the trauma by attempting to find minimal amounts of order in the chaos. So, when she remembered it was trash day, she set aside her journal and pulled the trash bin to the curb, an action that might puzzle those unfamiliar with how trauma can work. "I was glad I went out," she said, "because I ended up finding my purse and the contents. So, you know, the benefits of being responsible," she said with a smile. "My cash was gone, but all the cards were there."

Her children began to wake, and Rachel did everything she could to keep things normal. She made breakfast all the while trying to think of what she could tell them that would speak the truth while minimizing the trauma. An episode of the children's show "Adventures in Odyssey" came to mind where a family wakes up on Christmas morning to discover all of their gifts had been stolen. Rachel reminded the children of that story and then proceeded to tell them that something similar had happened to them—that their house had been robbed. Rachel told them to remember the story. She encouraged them to remember the ending—to remember that in the end everything is okay. The family is safe and they are together. She talked to her children in a manner they could comprehend and took them through the story, all the way up to the end allowing them rest in the peace of that narrative. "I think God gave that idea to me," Rachel states.

After breakfast, she loaded up her children in the van and drove to where her husband was staying. The conversation that ensued was a difficult one. The children encountered their father in the hallway and announced they had been robbed. As the children filled Simon in on the details they were privy to, the gravity and implications of what they were saying washed over him. When he realized his wife had actually *seen* the men he pulled Rachel to the side.

In that moment, one of the hardest parts for Rachel was knowing how to communicate the truth of what happened. She had sworn to the men that she wouldn't tell anyone.

> I firmly believe in truth-telling even in the situation when it's easy to lie or it feels justified. . . . The men that broke in said that if I told anybody what happened that night, they would come back and kill the kids. So that was one of the things I wrestled with when I was lying on the couch that night. Whenever you watch a movie, you think *"Go to the cops!"* Even though they tell you not to. It makes the most sense to go to the cops. But I told those guys that I wouldn't tell and swore to God that I wouldn't tell. So, when Simon asked, it was hard for me to answer. I told Simon to ask me "Yes or No" questions. And so, he did. . . . Being able to say "Yes" or "No" was easier than saying what they did. He called the cops and we met them there and the day began.

As one might expect, Rachel's day consisted of walking officers through her house, medical examinations, and answering many, many questions.

That night Rachel and Simon decided they would never stay in that house again. Rachel recalls the next few days as "living in a sadness . . . not knowing how you should be responding." They entrusted themselves to the care of friends and family, shifting from spare rooms to guest houses to campers, any place where they could be surrounded by loved ones. It was in these places that Rachel gathered with family and dear friends to discuss practical steps of what would come next. What would they do with the house? The car? What was the family's options in terms of therapy? Rachel speaks of small, tangible acts of care in those early days:

> We were able to stay at some friends' house and the next day I wanted to just lie on the couch. And they said I needed to lie down to rest. But every time I would close my eyes, I'd see a penis. I didn't want to close my eyes. And just the little things they did for me, they brought me water and granola and it was so good and tasted delicious and so she made more. And she came and massaged my shoulders. I don't think they tried to talk other than asking little questions checking in on me. But it wasn't like, "Let's try to talk out why this happened."

Rachel spoke of wanting to avoid the people who early on wanted to discuss with her the "whys" behind this incident. "Because you don't really care *why* it happened yet. You're just thinking, 'My back hurts' or 'Go watch the kids,'" because I couldn't deal with that at the moment.

In these acts of care, Rachel experienced the recognition of others. Recognition was not dependent on knowing the details of the assault. In fact, recognition in this case meant giving space to *not* speak of the details if Rachel so chose.

A former professor of Rachel's invited her and her family to stay with them while they attempted to piece their lives back together. Rachel is an interior designer, as was the professor who opened up her house. "It was a beautiful home," Rachel explained. "It was well-designed so I was in heaven," she continued, nodding to the transcendence of beauty.

It was while they were staying at this house when they received two surprising phone calls. The first was a friend telling them that an anonymous donor wanted to buy them any house of their choosing. A few hours later a different friend called and said they wanted to buy Rachel and Simon's current house so that they wouldn't have to deal with the details of putting it on the market. "So that was very humbling," Rachel explained.

> By the end of that day, we were pretty floored. God was taking care of us through other people which I think, I've known that before, but when you go through something, it definitely makes it real to you like, people are the hands and feet of Christ. And sometimes they probably do it without knowing it; it's not like God is saying to each one "Go and do this for me." They might think it's their thought. But I really do think that God uses that to show us he loves us.

A generous family from their church invited Rachel's family to stay at their extensive ranch for a week. The ranch was large enough that it could house Rachel's extended family as well and they experienced somewhat of a family reunion.

Remarkably, the week Rachel's family was there happened to overlap with the caretaker's son and daughter-in-law's annual visit. The caretaker's children visited the ranch for one week every summer. Janie and Rob introduced themselves to Rachel and Simon and shared how ten years ago, Janie had been raped in her own home. These were the first people Rachel and Simon spoke with who seemed to have a deep understanding of what they had experienced. The two couples sat down to talk. Rachel explains:

> It was so cool. Just the things that they put into words, especially because they're ten years out looking back, they had such a different perspective. The biggest one that stands out, they brought up the point that we're probably only thinking about our life . . . like our life started July 15, 2014. I hadn't been thinking of anything prior to that. Everything was starting that day. And everything has been since then. And I was like, "You're right! I haven't been thinking about anything else in my life. Everything is just about that day and after." So, bringing that into the light was like "Ok my circle is really small right and it will grow over time and eventually I'll remember what happened before that day."

Rachel sees the hand of God in orchestrating the meeting with Janie. Even as she describes this encounter years later, her face lights up.

Rachel's family bounced around visiting with family and friends until their new house was ready. All throughout this period, Rachel speaks of people in the community, strangers and friends alike, sending the family money through the mail. Rachel shares how people in the community packed up their entire house and moved everything for them. "We didn't have to do anything." She said. "It was amazing. Such a gift, and so we moved in and then I started painting and organizing. The kids think now that if you get robbed, you get a new house," she said with a smile.

Money in the mailbox and the gift of a new house alone did not heal the wounds of trauma. Rachel speaks of triggers of meeting men and their holding out hands to shake. She describes the terrifying and confusing experience of a family member jokingly threatening to throw her into a pool. And this was all on top of the fear that the men might come back. Rachel worried about them recognizing her family van. "Everywhere I drove, I felt like they were following me. I was always on the lookout. I would go to soccer games and think 'Are they here somewhere?' We ended up getting a new van and that made us all feel a little bit safer because they had used our van while they were at our house." She cut her hair to alter her appearance. "It seems silly looking back, but you don't know at the time."

About two months after the attack, Rachel and her family were at a community water park. Rachel was in a swimsuit and cover-up and found herself struggling with her thoughts on other's perceptions: "I remember thinking, 'When people see me, are they going to think, *I would have raped that too?'* Everybody's going to be thinking of my body in that context."

That Christmas Rachel and Simon went on a cruise where she encountered a number of men that fit the description of the assailants. Rachel shared how it seemed as if every single one of them knew exactly what had happened to her and somehow were also responsible for those events. "Just connecting them in that way which obviously isn't true. But just those connections your brain makes," Rachel explains. "There was one instance where someone introduced me to their friend and he was a teenager who fit the description and he shook my hand and I didn't want to touch him. I shook back, but it wasn't pleasant at all . . . I couldn't take my eyes off of his hands."

Rachel also dealt with shame wondering why she didn't fight back and what might have happened if she had. Throughout all of this were the disorienting questions concerning the presence and providence of God. She speaks of going back to church soon after the attack and singing a song with the line, "You're my defender."

"I got a huge frog in my throat like how do I deal with that? You didn't defend me that night. But God has different ways. Maybe he did. He didn't stop it completely though."

Her theological wrestling is worth exploring at length:

> I go back and forth between, "Is God involved in everyday little details of the physical things in my life?" Like losing my keys? "Lord help me find them. Oh, they're in my fridge, I forgot." I go back and forth between "How would God care about my keys if children are starving and they pray for food and don't get it and die?" . . . That's a huge spectrum. The more I think about it, the worse it gets. And I just don't want to think about it anymore. So somewhere I fall on that spectrum of what happened to me and God knew it was going to happen. But still, I guess the easiest way to put it is that God knew it was going to happen, prevented certain things like the children sleeping, the attackers not beating or killing me. Maybe they weren't going to do that anyway. Allowing them to make decisions because we have our freewill. But protecting my innocent children in the midst of it and then prompting people in the body of Christ to pour out his love on us afterwards . . . I feel like I've been blessed for what I endured and for whatever reason, God has allowed those blessings to be poured out. Compensating for what I went through. And my children were protected. I feel like it's the happiest ending and I don't know why. If I had to go back, it sounds kind of awful to say it, but I'm thankful that it happened because of how good everything has turned out. Like when I go back and think where we would be if it hadn't happened, and it's like, I love where we're at now and love what has happened since then. I don't know how you. . ."

Rachel's voice trailed off at this point, unsure of how to proceed. Rachel's articulation of God's presence came haltingly. There was a continual struggle to understand the presence of evil in the world. Is she allowed to enjoy her life knowing that many of the blessings received sprung out of horrific circumstances? While speaking of the gifts from the community, Rachel vocalizes her questions:

> I kind of wrestle with it because they are material physical blessings. Why does God care about that? There are people struggling who don't have food around the world. Why would he provide a house to me when there is someone down the street who is losing theirs because they can't pay for it? Why does God help some and not others? I don't know. It turns sticky quick. So, I try not to think about that and just say, "Thank you God for what was provided."

Rachel chooses over and over again to take the path of gratitude over cynicism, simply articulating her gratitude to God.

Within a few weeks of the attack, Karen reached out to Rachel's husband, Simon, and offered to take Rachel to see Felicia, the trauma therapist. Rachel was amenable to the idea, so Karen made the appointment, drove her to Indianapolis, and paid for her first session. The women were acquaintances at best at this point. They attended the same church and knew each other by name, but Karen was a widow with grown children and Rachel was a young mom with four small kids. While they did not seem to have a whole lot in common, their traumatic experiences served to bond them together.

Speaking of trauma therapy, Rachel confesses:

> I don't know how soon we would have sought it out on our own. But Karen said, "I want to take you." And I think that's really crucial. Because a lot of times, I'll *tell* someone else to go to counseling . . . But Karen *took* me there the first time. It meant a lot for her to do that, and I don't know if I would have pursued it that soon if she hadn't taken that step.

Two years after that first appointment, Karen confessed, "I thought 'This poor girl is thinking that she doesn't even know me and I'm dragging her down here . . . And she was gracious enough to insert my will upon her life [both Karen and Rachel laughed at this point] . . . I haven't been as forceful with anybody else."

The hour-and-a-half ride was spent discussing what Rachel might experience in her first session. They stuck with the more technical aspects of EMDR. Karen explained:

> I mostly didn't want to pry or make her feel like she owed me the story if she didn't want to. But mostly I just knew how invaluable that therapy was for me and I just pushed pretty hard that Rachel got down there. And I actually only took her once, but it was a privilege for me and Rachel's a pretty amazing person.[5]

Rachel reported finding trauma therapy to be both beneficial and validating. "This is actually a science," she explains.

> There are real things happening in my brain that weren't happening before, and it's going to process differently . . . it's actually physiological; your body has changed and it needs to be dealt with in a different way. Just the way Felicia explained it was so cool. Like just the way that your brain doesn't file these trauma things away and it's just floating around. Ready to react at any time if something might set it off.

Rachel was walking into a grocery store with her kids in tow when she received the news that her assailants had been identified and were going to be arrested that day. Detectives had found and tracked Rachel's stolen laptop and then matched hair, semen, and fingerprints left by all three perpetrators.[6] Video surveillance from the convenience store visited by two of the men was later used to identify the men.

That afternoon, police went to the local high school and arrested three young men for the crime. The knowledge that the suspects had been caught was a huge relief to Rachel, even changing the way that she walked around her house.

> We had a security system which was a huge relief. I had always said, "God is my security system, why do people need security systems?" But now I have one and I love it. It brought a lot of peace of mind having it. But even walking around sometimes, I would always look through the windows to see if anyone was out there. So just knowing that they were caught changed that and gave us more peace.

That peace, however, was mixed with sadness over the young age of the perpetrators. Rachel's compassion was remarkable:

> You feel sorry for them because they were so young. They didn't *act* young, but they *are* young. So, if it would have been someone like a peer or older, I think there would be a lot more anger or hatred. But when they're younger, it made it more like I pitied them because of the lives that they've lived and that . . . there's all these other factors to what's happened to them and they're acting out what they're living.

The men arrested were two 15-year-olds and a 17-year-old. All three pled innocent and were moved up to an adult court in light of the serious nature of the crime and at the recommendation of state psychiatrists. The case came to trial a year later, and, ironically enough, it landed on the exact same week Janie and her husband were in town for their annual visit to family at the ranch. Once again, Rachel was supported by the woman who had been in her shoes a decade earlier. Janie was the only person Rachel invited into the courtroom the day that she testified against the men. She explains:

> I didn't want my family to be there. But I asked her to be there because she could hear the nitty-gritty of things that happened. I didn't want my parents to hear the things that were done . . . (But they were all willing to of course, if I wanted them there) . . . I don't know Janie that well and we hardly ever talk, but she was important and played a role. It's just so neat how God had woven them into our lives in those little ways.

Even though Rachel was not particularly close to Janie, there was a mutual recognition of what the other had experienced. Interestingly enough, Janie's attacker was recently caught and she is preparing to go to trial. Rachel looks forward to returning the favor and supporting Janie during this time.

Rachel was not allowed in the courtroom except for her testimony and the closing arguments. And it was during the closing arguments that Rachel's anger peaked. The defense attorney had two goals: (1) demonstrate the rapists were too young to know their acts were not consensual and (2) discredit Rachel by attacking her character. The defense attorney's case began in his opening statements. He explained to the jury that the victim was a willing participant in the events and urged the jury to look at the facts of the case as opposed to the emotions of the case.[7] "They asked her to do things and she complied," the attorney said. "She does nothing at first after the three suspects left; instead of immediately reporting the crime she does nothing."[8]

Rachel explains that she had more anger toward the lawyer than she did for the perpetrators. "I was about to stand up and lose it on this guy," she said. "I went home that day and just laid on my bed and was so exhausted just from listening to that. I couldn't sleep. All I could do for so long was just lay there and think about what I wanted to say to that man. He didn't even do it, but he got added in [with] the other three. He was on the list. He didn't do the act, but if he was going to say all those things, it felt like he did."

Social media was a buzz around that time with friends and family of the three young men spreading stories of a young woman who only "cried rape" when her husband found out. The shared sentiment among this contingency was, *if you knew the whole story, you wouldn't feel so bad for that woman.*

Ultimately, all three men were convicted of multiple felonies and sentenced to 40 years in prison and Rachel joined the relatively small ranks of sexually assaulted women who were actually believed, and the even smaller ranks of sexually assaulted women whose perpetrators go to prison. And with that decision came a formal recognition from the American court system concerning the trauma Rachel had experienced. It was a legal recognition backing up the veracity of Rachel's testimony.

SHARING STORIES

On a Sunday evening Rachel came to my house to share her story with the young women who were a part of the anonymous support group at my house. They listened to Rachel's story of pain and healing and had the opportunity to ask delicate and pressing questions. I had invited Rachel because hers is a story that has within it threads of hope. Women asked questions about whether or not her husband still loved her, and if she thought it was possible to be in any kind of loving relationship following abuse. Her story gave an infusion of hope.

And yet, it was also because of those threads of hope that make it a difficult story for some of the women to hear. The questions and comments that emerged after Rachel left that evening were sobering. The women shared things like "I kind of wish that had happened to me," "I wish people believed me," "I wish I could win in court like she did," "I hope I can find a spouse who won't be turned off by my past," and "Her story is so much worse than mine so why does she seem like she's coping better than me?"

The women were not craving the physical manifestations of support (money in mailboxes, new houses, etc.), they longed for the kind of *recognition* Rachel received. The nature of Rachel's trauma was such that it was known publically. Hiding something like this would have been difficult. But many of these young women could count on one hand the number of people who were aware of their situations. While there were a small handful who questioned the veracity of Rachel's testimony (friends and family of the perpetrators), the overwhelming consensus, backed by the court systems, was that Rachel's words were true. And not only were her words recognized as true, the consequences of that belief meant that the men were punished and that Rachel was gifted by the community with various items to help her rebuild her life.

And it's here that we introduce a key component in the act of recognition: that of *redistribution*.[9] Recognition is more than just acknowledgment. There are situations in which in order to properly recognize someone there is the tandem act of redistribution.[10] In Rachel's case, it took the jury eight hours to find the first man guilty. Imagine, now, if at the later sentencing hearing the presiding judge acknowledged the guilt of the men and then released them back to the streets. Or imagine if Rachel did not have the support system she did have and was still living in the house where she was attacked, without any kind of security system, driving the family van which had been taken by the men, and all of this without ever having experienced any kind of trauma therapy. Even if the men were caught and imprisoned, if every other single aspect of Rachel's life remained the same, I wonder what her healing process would look like.

Rachel's story is an anomaly. Not because rape is uncommon, in actuality, the statistics concerning women and sexual assault are staggering. What is anomalistic is that (1) the community rallied behind Rachel and her family and (2) the men were caught and given lengthy sentences. The anomaly in Rachel's story is not the trauma; the anomaly is the recognition her story received.

Even now, two years after the attack Rachel is still in awe of the communal recognition. Rachel had a solid group of friends and was not surprised by the wonderful support they offered. Nor was she surprised by the way the pastors at her church loved and supported her (Rachel is a pastor's daughter herself and laughed as she explained it was their *job* to care). What did surprise Rachel were the people who cared for her who had seemingly no reason to do so—strangers and acquaintances.

> I think in general I was so humbled by how many people did say things and send cards, like, *why do people care so much?* And it was just very humbling for me to feel like people are taking the time to write me a note or sending us money. That's so kind. I'm so grateful, but also just in awe that people cared so much. . . . It was other people that don't know me . . . that just came out of the woodwork to encourage and to just make sure that you're doing ok or to write to you. And I think that's why it's more humbling because they're not your close friends. It really lifted me up.

Rachel was moved by the people that would approach her and say they had prayed for her in the middle of the night. I was struck by the beauty and vulnerability of what Rachel said next:

> I remember people from all throughout my life and the parts that they've played in my life, but I feel like no one else remembers me from theirs. Like I haven't made a difference in anyone's life and no one remembers me as a part of their life's story. And I know it's not true. But sometimes it feels like you haven't done anything memorable enough or haven't been close enough to people or they forget you or something. So, to have people say that they'd been thinking about me that week or praying for me or they thought of me yesterday. It was like, *Oh my goodness they thought of me when I wasn't in front of them!* It's special, it makes me feel good. I try to remember that with other people. *I was thinking about you and wanted to write.* Those things matter.

All of these experiences have had a major influence in the way Rachel desires to recognize others. When she recommends the trauma therapy she receives, she finds herself wondering, "Am I willing to drive this person? Or pay for this person to go?" She is keenly aware of others in the church who have experienced trauma. "A baby died recently, and when I see [the parents] at church . . . I can't just walk by." And so, Rachel stops, hugs them, tells them she is praying, and walks away.

RECOGNIZING LIMITS

Rachel speaks of the pressure many of us feel to try to fix or help a person who has experienced trauma. "I think back to what helped me," she says, "and it wasn't someone trying to help me. It was just them saying that they care. So . . . [when] my brain is racing trying to figure out what to say, I'm like, 'Stop! Just give them a hug and tell them they're loved and you'll be thinking of them.'" She acknowledges the futile feeling of not being able to solve another's problems. "It's so hard just to hug them and walk away and feel like you left them in their pile of crap. Like, 'Oh sorry! I'm thinking about you from over here.' But it does mean a lot." Rachel confessed that her tendency when she sees someone hurting is to want "to be someone's one answer," meaning that she is now the cure-all for whatever the person is experiencing. "But when I think about my own story," Rachel says, "I'm like, 'No!' I mean Karen took me to counseling but it's not like she checked in on me every month. . . . But [she's] still a part of my story in a really important way. . . . It's hard for me to remember that you don't have to be best buddies with everyone who is grieving . . . you trick yourself into thinking you have to be everyone's savior."

As my interview with Rachel was coming to an end, I asked if there was anything else we hadn't covered that she wanted to talk about. There was a long pause, and then Rachel haltingly brought up something that had been troubling her. She shared briefly of a dear friend whose father had recently been imprisoned for molesting a young boy.

Speaking of her friend's experience Rachel said, "That whole thing has been so much more difficult to deal with than what we've gone through." Rachel's words startled me and I leaned in as she attempted to explain her analysis. She proceeded to charge me with a task:

> I would be interested in you seeking out maybe as you look into this is the church and their response to sexual predators in the church. Because my friend is in the situation now where she is trying to forgive her father and move on, but they're such outsiders in the church so they feel rejected by everyone. . . . Hearing my friend's laments is hard and I don't know what to tell her. She has experienced a trauma because she was lied to by someone she loved and everything came crashing down.

Rachel acknowledged the shame that accompanies this kind of sexual sin: "It's such a private thing and you don't want to tell people . . . so they don't tell people and then they don't get help. My experience was so public, people I don't even know were being supportive of me. But for them, unless they tell people, they can't get help." The tension in Rachel's words was evident—if we tell people, we risk being ostracized. However, if we don't tell people we miss out on potentially healing relationships. "There's no place for them," Rachel says.

Rachel and I wrapped up the interview, and as I walked away from the coffee shop where we met I was struck by the concern Rachel expressed for this family. Perhaps the concern and compassion Rachel expressed stems from the deep form of recognition she received for her own pain. I wonder if Rachel would have the same concern for this family had she not received the love and support from her community. My hunch is that the love Rachel received from those around her was what allowed her to love those who might have otherwise been considered unlovable.

About a year after the attack, Rachel chose to share her story at a women's retreat. When I asked if it was difficult to share her story with such a large community she claimed she thought it would be more difficult to *not* share it with her community. She quoted the verse from Revelation 12:11 where evil is overcome "by the blood of the lamb and the word of their testimony." Rachel spoke of her own hope and healing that came through sharing her story and then added, "there's something spiritually that happens that we don't see that breaks some kind of chain."

CONCLUSION

Next month marks the fourth anniversary of this trauma. Rachel's life looks different. She's moved to a new state, and her family has grown. What hasn't changed, however, is her desire to share her story of hope. In our last interview, I made a comment about not wanting to "use" Rachel's story. She interrupted me and told me she *wanted* me to use it. Otherwise, she wondered, what's the point of the pain? She continued:

> It's meant to be shared or used in a way that other people can then learn something from what you went through. Give them some kind of hope. And I feel like that's definitely been true for me, about sharing and the healing that comes from that. And that's the purpose of being in that body of believers. I think is to give you a safe place to do that.

Rachel was not making a normative statement, nor was she defining "used" in the pejorative. Part of what it meant to recognize Rachel was to give her space to share her story as she so desired. It was her story. Which also meant it was hers to share. Rachel does not need well-intended but patronizing friends who try to protect her by avoiding certain topics. Instead, she desires relationships that create space for her to narrate her own story where and how she chooses. Because in Rachel's experience, testifying to her experience helped direct her towards a path of healing and freedom.

NOTES

1. Larenz Jordan v. State of Indiana. Court of Appeals No: 27A02-1511-CR-1897 (Court of Appeals of Indiana, 2016), 13.
2. Larenz Jordan v. State of Indiana. Court of Appeals No: 27A02-1511-CR-1897 (Court of Appeals of Indiana, 2016), 1–13.
3. Rachel. Interview by Amanda Hontz Drury. Digital Recording. Marion, IN, 8 July, 2016. All subsequent quotations from Rachel are from this interview.
4. Journal, shared with permission from author.
5. Karen and Rachel, Interview, 2016.
6. Marion Chronicle Tribune July 23, 2015.
7. Marion Chronicle Tribune July 23, 2015.
8. Marion Chronicle Tribune July 23, 2015.
9. See Butler on reciprocal recognition: "This temporality of discourse disorients one's own. Thus, it follows that one can give and take recognition only on the condition that one becomes disoriented from oneself by something which is not oneself, that one undergoes a de-centering and 'fails' to achieve self-identity." Butler, *Giving an Account*, 42.
10. In *Justice Interruptus*, Nancy Fraser develops a theory of justice that requires both recognition and redistribution, claiming that while the two are distinct, one is not irreducible to the other—they are interrelated. Nancy Fraser, *Justice Interruptus: Critical Reflections on the "Postsocialist" Condition* (New York: Routledge, 1996).

Theological Interlude 5
Running

> *So Peter and the other disciple started for the tomb. Both were running, but the other disciple outran Peter and reached the tomb first. He bent over and looked in at the strips of linen lying there but did not go in. Then Simon Peter came along behind him and went straight into the tomb. He saw the strips of linen lying there, as well as the cloth that had been wrapped around Jesus' head. The cloth was still lying in its place, separate from the linen. Finally the other disciple, who had reached the tomb first, also went inside. He saw and believed.*
>
> —John 20:3-8

There is a lot of running in this passage. We see a kind of competitive jostling between the two disciples: "Both were running, but the other disciple outran Peter and reached the tomb first." And then a few verses later, this other disciple reminds us again of his first-place arrival. Let it be clear! The other disciple made it to the tomb before Peter!

We may roll our eyes at the competitive slant of this Easter morning arrival. Come on, boys, does it really matter who outran whom? This race may seem silly to some of us, but it is perhaps a race in which we all compete. We are so inclined to compare our running with others. When we are left to work out our salvation with fear and trembling, we are tempted to measure our spirituality by comparing it to another's. *Am I running in the right direction? Am I keeping up? Is this the most effective form of training? Is this how Jesus would run? How's my breathing?* We run while glancing to our left and our right.

Peter and John are not the only players to run in this scene. Mary runs as well. Mary does not run *to* the tomb; however, Mary runs *from* the tomb. The tomb is barren and Mary hightails it back to the disciples.

Three players in this scene, and all three run differently: the one who runs from the tomb, the one who hesitates at the tomb, and the one who charges inside the tomb. All three will experience the same risen Lord despite their stride.

We all encounter the risen Lord differently—running, weeping, fleeing, and hesitating. We all experience the same risen Lord from different angles. These players are not ranked in their running. There is no ideal formulaic path to the tomb. The risen Lord appears to all without holding back. None of the players earned the right to gaze upon Jesus. Jesus simply appears in the midst of their run regardless of their direction. He just appears. This should make us all breathe a bit easier. If death could not hold Jesus down, then certainly hesitancy is not an unsurmountable barrier.

We encounter the true God differently. We respond to this God differently. It scares some of us half to death. Others grasp the significance of the meaning without being sure they actually believe it. Still others claim faith without really understanding what is at stake. Running for us is faith seeking understanding. Running is our plea for perfect love to cast out fear. And as we run, we know we do not run alone. There is, in fact, another who runs. There is another person with an undignified gait. Of course, this person is not a fellow disciple but the father himself who has spotted the bowed head of his prodigal child. The father runs.

The path to the father may be narrow, but it is not uniform. Whether we run headlong, whether we hesitate, whether we, in fact, take a few steps backward, this narrow path ultimately leads to a father who is running toward us, arms open.

Conclusion

CHRISTMAS DAY, 2014

Gifts were opened, food was eaten, and Sam and Clara were finally asleep in their beds. I noticed something sticking out from my previously emptied stocking. A journal. Inside was a loving and thoughtful note from my husband, John. I was not happy. "Why would he give me a journal? He knows I hate journaling. Did he forget about my experience with journaling the previous summer? Is this supposed to be a joke?" John is a morning person, and I am a night owl, so I was still fuming long after he had fallen asleep that night.

As I (angrily) prepared for bed that evening, I remembered something my mother-in-law had told me a few weeks before my wedding. "The best time to write your husband a love letter is when you're angry with him."

It seemed like bad advice. Hallmark movie advice. Nevertheless, I decided I would go through the motions of letter writing. I remember thinking, "I'm not writing a journal entry, I'm writing a letter." And so I began to write. I responded to John's thoughts about the upcoming year. I shared some of my own hopes, and I ended with a passage from The Book of Wisdom appropriate for Christmas:

When peaceful silence lay over all,
and when night had run halfway her swift course,
down from the heavens,
from the royal throne,
leapt your all-powerful
Word.

Book of Wisdom 18:14–15

I wasn't journaling, I was letter-writing, and poetry-quoting. I wrote a brief prayer, wished my husband a merry Christmas, and left the journal propped up near his morning vitamins.

John had already been awake for hours before I awoke the next morning. I opened my eyes, reached for my glasses on my end table, and saw the journal with an entry from 5:30 am. He wrote me back. That night I responded. We continued to pass the journal back and forth—I wrote prior to going bed, John wrote when he awoke. After a year and a half of silence, I was slowly easing back into the practice of journaling. There was something about writing with an audience (my husband) that made the practice more palatable.

This December will be seven years of nightly journaling with my husband. These journals have become a deep symbol of beauty and healing. That which was once a source of shame was transformed into a means of intimacy. One of the most painful aspects of my story was transformed into one of our most cherished practices. Our dry bones were dancing. There were streams in our wasteland.

Bibliography

Agamben, Giorgio. *Remnants of Auschwitz: The Witness and the Archive.* New York: Zone Books, 1999.

Amaresha, Anekal C., and Ganesan Venkatasubramanian. "Expressed Emotion in Schizophrenia: An Overview." *Indiana Journal of Psychological Medicine* 34, no. 1 (2012): 12–20.

American Psychiatric Association. *Diagnostic and Statistical Manual of Mental Disorders: DSM-IV-TR.* Washington, DC: American Psychiatric Association, 2000.

Barth, Karl. *Church Dogmatics* II/1. Edinburgh: T & T Clark, 1957.

———. *Church Dogmatics* III/2. London: T & T Clark, 2009.

Beiser, Frederick. *Hegel.* New York: Routledge, 2005.

Blow, Charles M. "The Whole System Failed Trayvon Martin," The New York Times, July 15, 2013. Accessed October 13, 2016. http://www.nytimes.com/2013/07/16/opinion/the-whole-system-failed.html?_r=0.

Bowler, Kate. *Everything Happens for a Reason and Other Lies I've Loved.* New York: Random House, 2018.

Brown, Sharon Garlough. *Sensible Shoes: A Story about the Spiritual Journey.* Downers Grove, IL: InterVarsity Press, 2013.

Brown, Robert McAfee. *Unexpected News: Reading the Bible with Third World Eyes.* Philadelphia: Westminster Press, 1984.

Brueggemann, Walter. "Reading From the Day 'In Between.'" In *A Shadow of Glory: Reading the New Testament after the Holocaust,* edited by Tod Linafelt. New York: Routledge, 2002.

Bryant, Jennings, and Dolf Zillmann. "Empathy: Affect from Bearing Witness to the Emotions of Others." In *Responding to the Screen, Reception and Reaction Processes,* 135–168. Hillsdale, NJ: L. Erlbaum Associates, 1991.

Butler, Judith. *Giving an Account of Oneself.* New York: Fordham University Press, 2005.

———. *Senses of the Subject.* New York: Fordham University Press, 2015.

Drury, Amanda. *Saying is Believing: The Necessity of Testimony in Adolescent Spiritual Formation*. Chicago: InterVarsity Press, 2015.

Duff, N.J., and G.S. Mikoski. "On the Complexities of Forgiveness". *Theology Today* 69, no. 4 (2013): 381–384.

Fraser, Nancy. *Justice Interruptus: Critical Reflections on the "Postsocialist" Condition*. New York: Routledge, 1996.

Fraser, Nancy, and Axel Honneth. *Redistribution and Recognition: A Political-Philosophical Exchange*. London: Verso, 2003.

Grosz, Elizabeth. *Becoming Undone: Darwinian Reflections on Life, Politics and Art*. Durham, NC: Duke University Press, 2011.

Herman, Judith Lewis. *Trauma and Recovery*. London: Pandora, 2015.

Hoffman, Martin L., "A Three Component Model of Empathy" (Paper presented at the Biennial Meeting of the Society for Research in Child Development, New Orleans, Louisiana, March 17–20, 1977). This paper is available on microfiche at http://files.eric.ed.gov/fulltext/ED139514.pdf, accessed November 21, 2016.

Hong, Howard V., and Edna H. Hong. *The Essential Kierkegaard*. Princeton: Princeton University Press: 2000.

"How Black Can Black Be?" *BBC Radio 4's Today Programme*. Transcript, September 23, 2014. Accessed August 12, 2016. http://www.bbc.com/news/entertainment-arts-29326916.

Hunsinger, Deborah van Deusen. *Bearing the Unbearable: Trauma, Gospel, and Pastoral Care*. Grand Rapids, MI: Eerdmans, 2015.

"Hyperlink Cinema and the Presence of Intertwining Stories." The Artiface. Accessed October 16, 2017. https://the-artifice.com/hyperlink-cinema-stories/.

Jones, Serene. *Trauma and Grace: Theology in a Ruptured World*. Louisville, KY: Westminster John Knox Press, 2009.

Joseph, Abson Prédestin. *A Narratological Reading of 1 Peter*. London: T. & T. Clark, 2012.

Karen. Interview by Amanda Hontz Drury. Digital recording. Marion, IN. 25 May 2016.

Karen and Rachel Peterson. Interview by Amanda Hontz Drury. Digital recording. Marion, IN. 25 August 2016.

Keen, Suzanne. "A Theory of Narrative Empathy." *Narrative* 14, no. 3 (Oct. 2006): 207–36.

Laitinen, Arto. "Interpersonal Recognition: A Response to Value or Precondition of Personhood." *Inquiry* 45 (2002): 463–78.

Larenz Jordan v. State of Indiana. Court of Appeals No: 27A02-1511-CR-1897. Court of Appeals of Indiana, 2016.

Lewis, C.S. *A Grief Observed*. New York: Harper One, 1961.

Markell, Patchen. *Bound by Recognition*. Princeton: Princeton University Press, 2003.

McNay, Lois. *Against Recognition*. Cambridge: Polity, 2008.

Miller, Lulu. "The Problem with the Solution" in Invisibilia, Podcast transcript. July 6, 2016. Accessed February 19, 2018. https://www.npr.org/2016/07/01/483856025/read-the-transcript.

Rachel. Interview by Amanda Hontz Drury. Digital Recording. Marion, IN, 8 July 2016.

Rambo, Shelly. "Resurrecting Scars." Feminism and Religion. Last modified April 9, 2012. https://feminismandreligion.com/2012/04/09/resurrecting-scars-by-shelly-rambo/.

———. *Resurrecting Wounds: Living in the Afterlife of Trauma*. Baylor, TX: Baylor University Press, 2017.

———. *Spirit and Trauma: A Theology of Remaining*. Louisville, KY: Westminster John Knox Press, 2010.

Rich, Adrienne. "Invisibility in Academe" *Blood, Bread and Poetry*. New York: Norton, 1986.

———. *On Lies, Secrets, and Silence: Selected Prose 1966–1978*. New York: Norton, 1979.

Root, Andrew. *Revisiting Relational Youth Ministry: From a Strategy of Influence to a Theology of Incarnation*. Downers Grove: InterVaristy Press, 2007.

Rothschild, Babette. *The Body Remembers: The Psychophysiology of Trauma and Trauma Treatment*. New York: Norton, 2000.

Sarah. Interview by Amanda Hontz Drury. Digital recording. Marion, IN. 20 May 2016.

Taylor, Charles. *Ethics of Authenticity*. Boston: Harvard University Press, 1992.

———. *Multiculturalism: Examining the Politics of Recognition*. Princeton, NJ: Princeton University Press, 2011.

Tolstoy, Leo. *Anna Karenina*. Oxford: Oxford World's Classics, 2016.

Trible, Phyllis. *Texts of Terror: Literary Feminist Readings of Biblical Narratives*. Minneapolis: Fortress Press, 1984.

Van der Kolk, Bessel A. *The Body Keeps Score: Integration of Mind, Brain, and Body in the Treatment of Trauma*. Phoenix, AZ: Milton H. Erickson Foundation, 2013.

Weingarten, Kaethe. *Common Shock: Witnessing Violence Every Day*. New York: Dutton, 2003.

Wells, Karin. "Psychiatric Community Care: Belgium Town sets the Gold Standard," Canadian Broadcasting Corporation. Accessed September 11, 2017. http://www.cbc.ca/news/world/psychiatric-community-care-belgian-town-sets-gold-standard-1.2557698 .

Williams, Robert R. *Recognition: Fichte and Hegel on the Other*. Albany, NY: State University of New York Press, 1992.

Williams, Robert R. *Hegel's Ethics of Recognition*. Berkeley: University of California Press, 2000.

Williams, Rowan. *Resurrection: Interpreting the Easter Gospel*. London: Darton, Longman & Todd, 1982.

Winnicott, Donald. "Fear of Breakdown," *International Review of Psychoanalysis* 1 (1974): 103–07.

Woman 1, surveyed by author, 14 February 2014, Marion, digital record. Indiana Wesleyan University, Marion, Indiana.

Woman 2, surveyed by author, 16 February 2014, Marion, digital record. Indiana Wesleyan University, Marion, Indiana.

Woman 3, surveyed by author, 16 February 2014, Marion, digital record. Indiana Wesleyan University, Marion, Indiana.

Woman 4, surveyed by author, 16 February 2014, Marion, digital record. Indiana Wesleyan University, Marion, Indiana.

Woman 5, surveyed by author, 17 February 2014, Marion, digital record. Indiana Wesleyan University, Marion, Indiana.

Woman 6, surveyed by author, 18 February 2014, Marion, digital record. Indiana Wesleyan University, Marion, Indiana.

Woman 7, surveyed by author, 1 March 2014, Marion, digital record. Indiana Wesleyan University, Marion, Indiana.

Index

Agamben, Giorgio, 7, 9–10
articulacy loop, 4–5, 14, 40–41, 73
articulation: as healing, 94; inadequacy of, 10–11, 72–73; of others, 30–34, 74; re-articulation, 11, 33; theory of, 4–5, 9–12, 29, 74. See also identity formation

Barth, Karl, 15n2, 17n31
Beiser, Frederick, 6, 16n7
Bible: Hagar's story, 43; John 20, 79–80, 97–98; lament texts, 48; Lazarus, 61–62; Mark's Gospel ending, 21–22; promises of God, 69–71, 76, 86; texts of trauma, 32, 47–48
Blow, Charles M., 39–40
Bowler, Kate, 24n5
Brown, George, 35–36
Brown, Robert McAfee, 46n32
Brown, Sharon Garlough, 46n30
Brueggemann, Walter, 17, 19–20, 23n1, 24n2
Butler, Judith, 10–11, 16n20, 36–37, 41, 45n24, 45n27, 46n35, 74, 95n9

caring other/compassionate witness. See *specific* mutual recognition

church's role in recognizing trauma, 7, 47, 73

Eye Movement Desensitization and Reprocessing (EMDR), 54, 66, 88

fractured imagination, 15–16, 21. See *also* trauma, inability to integrate
Fraser, Nancy, 16n7, 44n6, 95n10

God: presence in trauma, 3, 23, 61–62, 80, 82–83; recognition by, 43; wrestling with, 43, 64, 69–71, 87

Hegel, 5, 6, 42, 16n7, 16nn9–10, 42
Herman, Judith Lewis, 16n15
Hofer, Johannes, 15–16n6
Holy Saturday, 29–23
Hong, Howard V. and Hong, Edna H., 44n5
Honneth, Axel, 16n7, 44n6
Hunsinger, Deborah van Deusen, 68–69, 77n6

identity formation, 5–6, 11, 24; Christian identity, 3, 70; mutual recognition and, 41–42; self-recognition and, 2–3, 30–31, 71

Jones, Serene, 3–4, 21–22, 23n1
Joseph, Abson, 25n16

Kapoor, Anish, 65
Keen, Susan, 45n18
Kierkegaard, Soren, 7, 29, 44n5

Laitinen, Arto, 44n9

McNay, Lois, 44n9

Patchen, Markell, 44n9
post-traumatic stress disorder, 8, 52–58

race, 38–39
Rambo, Shelly, 5, 15n6, 20–21, 23, 24n4, 25n17, 43n1, 48
recognition, 2, 6, 12–14, 32, 38–43, 68; forms of, 12, 34; misrecognition, 6, 30, 34, 40–41, 72; mutual recognition, 35–36, 68–76, 85–88; as presence, 37, 72, 79, 84–85; as redistribution, 91; rituals of, 28–30

Rich, Adrienne, 34, 45n19, 45n28
Root, Andrew, 45n26
Rothschild, Babette, 55, 60nn7–8

Taylor, Charles, 6, 11
testimony. *See* articulation
Tolstoy, Leo, 71
trauma: definition of, 9, 53; effect on the body, 2, 53–56, 66–67, 88; inability to integrate, 4–6, 43, 54–55, 88; recognition of, 2, 6, 29; traumatic event, 8–9, 49–53, 64–65
triggers, 2, 50–57, 66

Van der Kolk, Bessel A., 16n15
Vanta Black, 65

Watson, Lila, 42
Weingarten, Kaethe, 55–56
Williams, Robert, 6, 42, 46n32
Williams, Rowan, 23n1, 24n8
Winnicott, Donald, 65

About the Author

The Reverend **Amanda Hontz Drury** (PhD, Princeton Theological Seminary) is professor of Practical Theology at Indiana Wesleyan University where she teaches and oversees various grants. She serves as the head of Discipleship by Design as well as the Brain Kitchen. Amanda lives in Indiana with her husband, John, and their three children, Samuel, Clara, and Paul.

www.ingramcontent.com/pod-product-compliance
Lightning Source LLC
Chambersburg PA
CBHW061720300426
44115CB00014B/2764